Inside the Board Room

Reflections of a Former School Board Member

Howard Good

Rowman & Littlefield Education
Lanham, Maryland • Toronto • Oxford
2006

Published in the United States of America
by Rowman & Littlefield Education
A Division of Rowman & Littlefield Publishers, Inc.
A wholly owned subsidiary of The Rowman & Littlefield Publishing Group, Inc.
4501 Forbes Boulevard, Suite 200, Lanham, Maryland 20706
www.rowmaneducation.com

PO Box 317
Oxford
OX2 9RU, UK

Copyright © 2006 by Howard Good

All rights reserved. No part of this publication may be reproduced, stored in a retrieval system, or transmitted in any form or by any means, electronic, mechanical, photocopying, recording, or otherwise, without the prior permission of the publisher.

British Library Cataloguing in Publication Information Available

Library of Congress Cataloging-in-Publication Data

Good, Howard, 1951–
  Inside the board room : reflections of a former school board member / Howard Good.
    p. cm.
  ISBN-13: 978-1-57886-452-2 (hardcover : alk. paper)
  ISBN-10: 1-57886-452-6 (hardcover : alk. paper)
  ISBN-13: 978-1-57886-453-9 (pbk. : alk. paper)
  ISBN-10: 1-57886-453-4 (pbk. : alk. paper)
   1. Education—Aims and objectives—United States. 2. School boards—United States. I. Title.
  LA217.2.G663 2006
  370.1′531—dc22   2006004299

∞ ™ The paper used in this publication meets the minimum requirements of American National Standard for Information Sciences—Permanence of Paper for Printed Library Materials, ANSI/NISO Z39.48-1992. Manufactured in the United States of America.

In memory of my mom, Lillie Good

Contents

Preface — vii

Acknowledgments — ix

1. Top Ten — 1
2. Losing It — 3
3. Now Playing — 11
4. Not with a Bang — 17
5. Wilderness Road — 21
6. Graduation Day — 27
7. Honor Role — 31
8. A Darkness Darker Than Night — 37
9. Schoolhouse Rock — 41
10. Straight to Hell — 47
11. The Deepest Cut — 51
12. The Bard of Education — 55
13. These Truths — 61

14	"War Minus the Shooting"	65
15	The Finger	73
16	The Way of the Kayak	77
17	After Story Hour	79
18	Write and Wrong	83
19	Sing!	87
20	Board-dom	91

| About the Author | 97 |

Preface

After I lost my seat on the school board, people would ask me, "What are you going to do with all your free time?"—as if I were searching for a new hobby now that the fun of attendance at board meetings was over. I didn't know what to say, so I wouldn't say anything, just smile and shrug. In retrospect, I can see that I could have said, "Write a book," not that many would have found that commendable or even comprehensible.

Inside the Board Room: Reflections of a Former School Board Member is, as its subtitle suggests, a sequel to my collection of essays, *Educated Guess: A School Board Member Reflects* (ScarecrowEducation, 2003). Although I may have lost my seat on the board, I didn't suddenly lose my interest in the issues I faced for six years as a board member. To be honest, I felt like I was interrupted in mid-sentence when the voters spoke. This book is an attempt to complete my thought.

I hope readers will draw ideas and inspiration from it. But anyone who writes as much as I do here about the shortcomings of the school system risks being accused of negativism, cynicism, defeatism, and perhaps satanism. My daughter Darla, whom you will meet several times in the following pages, has developed a strategy for dealing with this kind of thing. When making what some might construe as a criticism, she always innocently adds, "I'm not complaining; I'm just telling."

Me, too.

Acknowledgments

Editors aren't always the easiest people for a writer to like. Sometimes it can seem that they were put on earth for the sole purpose of making you give up writing. So I consider myself extraordinarily lucky to have had my writing shepherded into print over the past eight years by Sally Banks Zakariya of *American School Board Journal*, Rich Shea and Mark Toner of *Teacher Magazine*, and Sandy Reeves of *Education Week*. Without their encouragement, this book probably wouldn't exist. About half the essays in it previously appeared in one or another of their publications. They are everything a writer could want in an editor: brave, smart, and sympathetic. And they don't mind paying you, either.

Chapter One

Top Ten

Maybe it has something to do with shrinking attention spans. Or maybe it's simply the inevitable result of America's years of exposure to the *Late Show* host David Letterman's "top ten" lists. Whatever the cause, a mania for lists seems to have overtaken the country. You can find lists on practically any subject online: the worst pop songs of all time (no. 1: "MacArthur Park"), the worst classic novels (anything by James Fenimore Cooper), or the worst jobs for teenagers (a tie between drug dealer and stripper). Now, in the same spirit of public service that once led me to sit on a school board, I offer a Letterman-like list of my own:

**THE TOP TEN SIGNS YOU'VE SERVED ON
THE SCHOOL BOARD TOO LONG**

10. You actually understand the provisions of the No Child Left Behind Act.
9. At board meetings, you find yourself increasingly tempted to get out of your chair, walk to the far end of the table, and twist like a doorknob the upper lip of a particularly opinionated fellow board member.
8. You try to think the same of all school administrators, i.e., badly.

7. You've begun to suspect that "curriculum mapping," which is taking your district longer than it took NASA to map the moon, may just be a clever euphemism for "futility."
6. You look forward to your next board meeting about as much as you would the telltale rash of a tick-borne disease.
5. You believe that if schools can't raise standards, they should at least lower the shades.
4. You have an idea for a new reality show—*Survivor! The Board–Superintendent Relationship*—in which board members put a superintendent through bogus and often grotesque challenges in an entertaining attempt to force her to resign.
3. You respect teachers; it's the fact they get paid that annoys you.
2. You just don't give a damn anymore how many snow days are left.
1. You chuckle malignantly to yourself whenever someone says, "I'm thinking about running for the school board."

Chapter Two

Losing It

I was standing in front of the education section at Barnes & Noble, scanning the tightly packed rows of books. As I read the titles—*High Schools on a Human Scale, Bridging the Achievement Gap, Why Is It So Hard to Get Good Schools?, Dumbing Us Down, Children as Pawns, Testing Is Not Teaching, Inventing Better Schools*—I was suddenly overcome with a vast weariness. I realized something I should have realized long before—the general futility of school reform efforts. Here were all these books, shelf upon crowded shelf of hardcovers and paperbacks, propounding dozens of ideas for school improvement, but, meanwhile, educational quality continued to slip. What had made me think my own efforts were somehow exempt from the law of entropy? How could I have been so naive?

No doubt this wasn't the best state of mind for me to be in, especially as I was trying to finish writing a book with the optimistic subtitle *Rediscovering the Aims of Education*. There were objective reasons, though, why my sense of optimism had collapsed like a Mideast truce. Perhaps the biggest was that only a few weeks earlier I had lost my bid for a third term on the school board. The defeat had left me feeling hurt and hollow and looking at the world with crusty eyes.

I hadn't really wanted to run again. After six years on the board, the last three as president, I had accumulated, along with political enemies and bad karma, the melancholy conviction that the stress and strain of board service outweighed the rewards. But I allowed myself to be persuaded by a few teachers, administrators, fellow board members, and neighbors that I was indispensable to the operation of the Highland Central School District. Vanity of vanities. I lost by fifty-four votes to a woman who used to give my kids piano lessons. It may be a measure of the nature of her influence that they now never touch the instrument.

Although I hated to lose, there were moments when I could almost accept my loss philosophically. I told myself that maybe the system was seeking equilibrium after the many changes the board had made during my tenure. We had added full-day kindergarten, Advanced Placement courses, art and music rooms, computers, an all-weather track, foreign language options, field trips, and more. Maybe my defeat wasn't so much a judgment on me personally—two other incumbents also lost—as the inevitable conservative reaction to the relentless pace of change. Maybe the community had reached the limit of what it expected from its schools or could spend on them and was about to take some needed rest.

This was a comforting theory, but, deep down, where anger and bitterness at my election loss still gnawed, I didn't believe it. Instead, I believed that I lost for random reasons: because the daily papers in the area didn't bother to cover the race or evaluate the candidates; because three of my opponents on the ballot banded together to hire a telemarketing firm to call all the voters in the district; because public hatred of school taxes, particularly the portion that goes to pay teachers' salaries, flared up; because critics of the superintendent had recently grown numerous, and when they took potshots at her, they often hit me, the board president, who sat beside her at meetings.

Why I lost the election is probably important only to me, but the consequences of a change in the makeup of a school board can affect thousands and last indefinitely. When a board turns over, you can't quickly right it, as you would a swamped kayak, with an Eskimo roll. What were once top priorities may end up stuck at the bottom, and efforts to improve this program or that school may be disrupted or even abandoned. The result is wasted resources, burned-out staff, unmet goals—in Seymour B. Sarason's telling phrase, "the predictable failure of educational reform."

Today when I look around my district, I see the previous board's initiatives in disarray. That is just how public education works—or, rather, why it doesn't. While my defeat was still fresh, first the superintendent resigned and then the high school principal, both fearful that the balance of power on the board had shifted irrevocably to the idiots, paranoids, and obstructionists. Their fears have proved justified. It took six years of grinding effort to move the district forward a fraction of an inch, but no time at all for things to slide far back beyond the point from which we had started.

The near impossibility of true educational reform has been documented in a number of studies. "If we have learned anything in recent decades," Sarason wrote, "it is that changing mission statements, curricula procedures, or laws in no way guarantees desired outcomes." Actually, some people haven't learned even this much yet, the New York State Board of Regents among them.

In 1996 the regents adopted a plan to raise academic standards statewide. The plan required that students pass tests in six subjects—English, mathematics, science, U.S. history, global studies, and a foreign language—in order to graduate from high school. The tests were to be introduced on a rolling basis, with the students entering ninth grade in 2001 the first to have to pass all six. Originally, the passing grade for the tests was 55, but it was to jump to 65 for the English, history, and global studies tests in 2004 and for the other tests in 2005.

Only a bunch of child-hating career bureaucrats in league with self-seeking politicians could possibly have come up with such a misconceived plan. Second thoughts about it arose almost immediately. A month after adopting the plan, the regents dropped the foreign language test as one of those needed for graduation. The test was, in the words of State Education Commissioner Richard Mills, a "bridge too far." Local school districts heaved a huge sigh of relief. They had always known, even if state ed. hadn't, that for most students foreign language proficiency meant having enough Spanish to be able to order from the drive-through menu at Taco Bell.

Other parts of the plan have also been revised in light of the performance of actual, rather than hypothetical, students. As 2004 approached, the regents announced that 55 would remain the passing grade on the required tests for at least another two years. Mills called the adjustment "a response to the data," giving an air of scientific rationality to what has become an out-of-control mess. The data showed that a whopping 9.9 percent of seniors statewide had scored between 55 and 64 on the tests. If the passing grade of 55 hadn't been extended, up to 20,000 students would have been ineligible to graduate in 2003.

The Math A test has caused the greatest carnage. It may have claimed more victims, proportionally speaking, than the bubonic plague during the Middle Ages. All twenty-two students in the Beacon City School District who took the test in June 2003 failed, even though twenty-one of them were passing the class. The dead wagon was piled just as high in many other districts.

To its credit, the state appointed a panel of mathematicians to review the test. The panel later issued a fifty-six-page report that recommended—you sitting?—publishing a suggested curriculum so teachers would know what to teach. If the decision makers at state ed. actually need a panel of experts to tell them something as obvious as this, we are worse off than I thought, and I already thought we were pretty much doomed to sizzle like sausages in the flames of some educational hell.

Publishing a suggested curriculum won't save us, but neither will ignoring the role of teachers in school reform. The studies all agree that, as one of them ungrammatically puts it, "teachers as change agents is the *sine qua non* of getting anywhere." School boards can meet late into the night; state ed. departments can raise standards; the federal government can require annual high-stakes testing. None of it will improve schooling as long as the daily interactions between teachers and students remain unchanged.

Much reform effort is designed to coerce changes in classroom practice, to overcome the perceived laziness or incompetence of teachers protected by tenure and inured to criticism. People may like their own kid's teacher well enough, but they tend to be suspicious of teachers as a group. Many don't even consider teaching real work, worthy of respect and a decent salary. It has been my experience that those who say they want to raise standards for students often just want to lower the boom on teachers.

Bad teachers certainly exist. Sometimes I think that I had most of them growing up and that my kids have had the rest. One morning while I was driving my daughter Darla, then an eighth grader, to school, she said, "You know, if they're gonna make us go to school for six hours a day, they could at least give us good teachers." What may have prompted this glum remark was an incident involving her band teacher.

Darla had been walking down a hall in the middle school when she saw a sixth grader drop her books and papers all over the floor. Although she had to pee, she stopped and helped the younger girl gather up her stuff. She made it to band just as the bell rang. When she asked the teacher if she could go to the bathroom, he shook his head. "You should've gone before class," he said. She tried to explain why she hadn't. He wouldn't listen. She sat all period squirming in her seat and fuming at the injustice done to her.

Ironically, the middle school operates a character education program, Project Wisdom, that is supposed to teach students old-fashioned virtues like kindness, honesty, and respect. What Darla learned that day in band was that the program is mere talk, that the adults at school are bullies and hypocrites, that it is safer to look out for yourself than to look out for others. This isn't anything a loving parent or a functioning school system would want a child to learn. But it is the very lesson the band teacher taught and the only one that, years later, Darla may remember from middle school.

Because school reformers are rarely intimately familiar with the culture of schools, they consistently underestimate the complexity of implementing their reforms. Character education, for example, is a fine idea, but that doesn't mean teachers will implement it as intended. They may not have the skills necessary to implement it, or the incentive, or the time. It is a long, hard, unpredictable journey from idea to implementation, and most reforms get lost, or at least roughed up and robbed, on the way. Sarason and other researchers have concluded that schools change reforms—through accommodation, resistance, hybridization—more than reforms ever change schools.

One oft-proposed solution involves attracting and retaining the kinds of teachers who can make a difference in children's lives. But where are we going to find these bright, motivated teachers? On eBay? Overseas? At schools of education, which typically have the lowest-achieving students on college campuses? And even if we did find them, could they do the job alone?

Of course not. As Ted Sizer of the Coalition of Essential Schools pointed out, "We are stuck with a school reform game in which any change affects all, where everyone must change if anything is to change." For reform to succeed, not only teachers must support it, but also parents, school boards, businesses, state legislatures, and the federal government. There must be money and organization to nurture it and patience to allow it to develop. The history of school reform in the United States can be read as one continuous cautionary tale about the futility of searching for quick fixes to complex problems. Those today who push the panacea of higher standards are hardly less ludicrous than the technophiles who, in the 1930s, pushed the panacea of instruction by movies and radio, never realizing that tens of thousands of rural schools had no electricity.

We shouldn't oversimplify the job of reforming schools. We

shouldn't confuse a change in policy with a change in practice. We shouldn't assume that adding more classroom computers or requiring more standardized tests will inevitably raise student achievement.

So what should we do? A few years ago David Tyack and Larry Cuban suggested "tinkering with the system," which they saw as "one way of preserving the valuable and reworking what is not." But most efforts at reform already constitute a kind of tinkering, now focusing on this problem, now on that, as if the system in which the problems emerge were basically sound. It isn't, and tinkering—which Webster's dictionary defines as "a clumsy attempt to mend something"—won't change that.

My own suggestion is that we blow the whole damn thing up and start over. You have seen news footage of old, decrepit buildings being instantly turned to rubble by implosion. Sometime during my second term on the school board, I began to entertain fantasies about similarly demolishing the system. I had served long enough by then to finally realize the truth, that certain problems were intractable and would never go away, that they were simply part of the standard operating procedures of schools. Now that I'm off the board and able to think more calmly, it is even clearer to me that the system can't be rehabilitated, only replaced, like a once-glamorous casino on the Las Vegas strip that disappears with an apocalyptic bang in a dark, boiling cloud of dust and debris.

Any volunteers to push the plunger?

REFERENCES

Fullan, Michael. *Change Forces: Probing the Depth of Educational Reform*. London: Falmer Press, 1993.

Sarason, Seymour B. *The Predictable Failure of Educational Reform: Can We Change Course before It's Too Late?* San Francisco: Jossey-Bass, 1990.

Sizer, Theodore. *The Red Pencil: Convictions from Experience in Education.* New Haven: Yale University Press, 2004.

Tyack, David, and Larry Cuban. *Tinkering toward Utopia: A Century of Public School Reform.* Cambridge, Mass.: Harvard University Press, 1995.

Chapter Three

Now Playing

Ever notice that when witnesses to a train wreck, fire, tornado, or other disaster are interviewed by the press, they often describe what they saw as having been "just like a movie"? Although make-believe, movies seem to increasingly provide the terms with which we define reality. Perhaps it isn't so strange, then, that I find myself using over and over again certain lines from movies as all-purpose responses to life's problems and riddles. I even wish now that during my six years on a local school board I had followed more closely the advice implicit in some of the lines that echo in my head. You might feel similarly once you hear them.

1. "Deserves" has nothing to do with it. So says Clint Eastwood, playing reformed outlaw William Munny in *Unforgiven*, winner of the Academy Award for best picture in 1992. Eastwood, gun drawn, is standing over Gene Hackman, playing sadistic lawman Little Bill Daggett, who lies wounded on the filthy floor of a squalid frontier saloon. Hackman has just protested that he doesn't deserve to die like this. Eastwood mutters the above line in reply, then pulls the trigger, pony-expressing Hackman's (or, rather, Little Bill's) rotten soul to hell.

Perhaps nowhere is the difference between what we deserve and what we get more starkly illustrated than in public education. School boards deserve adequate money to educate the young, but get cheated out of state and federal aid, burdened with unfunded mandates, and rebuffed by taxpayers. Teachers deserve support and cooperation from parents, but get treated like antagonists and accused of all sorts of lapses. Students deserve good schools, but get crowded into crumbling classrooms.

Cynicism can become second nature under these circumstances. I have seen it happen many times. A board member starts out filled with the innocent enthusiasm of a Pop Warner cheerleader, but then keeps crashing up against the constraints of the public education system—lack of resources, lack of coordination, lack of vision, lack of . . . you name it. The frustrated board member quits in the middle of a term, or worse, hangs around to make sure that everyone else is just as miserable as he or she is.

There is a better way, and it rests on the recognition that what we deserve on the job or in general has nothing to do with what we may end up getting. Once board members accept that, they can set achievable goals for themselves and their district. A mature, steady, realistic board is, after all, the very least that students deserve.

2. *What's the rumpus?* This is a question school board members would do well to ask. Tom Reagan (Gabriel Byrne), the chief lieutenant of a Prohibition-era crime boss in *Miller's Crossing*, poses it by way of greeting the various mugs, yeggs, and gunsels he encounters around town. He doesn't seem to expect an actual answer, but board members should. They are supposed to be informed when there is an uproar at the elementary school over field trips or a commotion at the high school over the student dress code.

But just because you ask, "What's the rumpus?" doesn't mean you will be told. It isn't that administrators will consciously lie to you. It is just that they have a natural tendency to put the best face on things. Their professional standing depends on maintaining the impression that they have the situation, no matter how far gone it is, under control.

Often my kids and their friends provided me with different information than what came in the weekly board packet. What's the rumpus? An unknown hooligan dropping cherry bombs down the toilets in the boys' room, rival girl gangs punching it out in the parking lot, teachers arguing with the principal in the hall. Kids will tell you if you ask. But, of course, given the badness of so much of the news, that isn't always easy to want to do.

3. *I wouldn't tie my shoes without a backup plan.* These words, spoken by jewel thief Joe Moore (the seemingly ubiquitous Gene Hackman) in writer-director David Mamet's *Heist*, should be kept continually in mind by board members. It is hard enough to improve school *with* a plan. Without a plan, it is close to impossible, like getting tenth graders to enjoy reading *The Scarlet Letter*.

At board meetings, I would hear a lot of good ideas for school improvement from administrators, teachers, the public, and even, on occasion, another board member. But having a good idea isn't the same as putting it into practice. A board should never approve an idea for change without first getting answers to the following questions: How much will it cost? How long will it take to implement? What are the specific objectives, and how and when will they be evaluated?

You may think these are simple questions that any administrator would be willing and able to answer, but some of the most stressful periods of my time on the board started with me asking for a plan. Perhaps the administrator lacked the expertise to draw up a real plan, one with a budget and timeline, or perhaps he (it was usually a he) just lacked the patience. Whatever the reason, the request would soon turn into a titanic battle, like something out of an old Godzilla movie. I always regretted this happening because of the danger that, as we grappled with each other, the community would be crushed underfoot.

4. *We're gonna need guns, lots of guns.* What Neo (Keanu Reeves) can be understood as saying in the first, and best, of *The Matrix* movies is that we need more than a plan of action. We also need the resources to execute it. A cross between messiah and male model, Neo is able to conjure up almost anything he needs on com-

mand. Guns? Whoosh! Long racks of chic-looking black machine guns instantly appear. Board members don't have that kind of power, but, boy, could they use it. Then when the state or federal government raised academic expectations for all students without comparably raising school aid, boards could just wish the extra aid into existence.

But why stop there? They could wish better school buildings, better textbooks, better teachers, better parents into existence, too. For the fact is, until districts have all or many of these things, the No Child Left Behind Act, with its peremptory demands for accountability and higher standards, is as much a fantasy as *The Matrix*, though not nearly as entertaining.

5. *Forget it, Jake—it's Chinatown.* The last line from the Academy Award–winning screenplay for *Chinatown* suggests that not every place has the same kind of culture or operates according to the same rules. This should serve as a reminder that what is educationally feasible in one community may be unfeasible in another. Although educational policy can originate far away, in Washington, D.C., or state capitals, it must be applied locally. And local conditions are notoriously uneven. A policy that works exactly as intended in the suburbs may not work at all in a rural district or the inner city.

My own experience on the school board showed me the futility of trying to override local conditions. When the board approved a summer reading program, for example, the outcry from parents was so great, you would have thought we had made miscegenation mandatory for all students. The board was hoping to raise reading scores on standardized tests as well as to cultivate young people's pleasure in books—goals for which the parents, who were mostly blue-collar types, felt little sympathy. To them, it was more important to keep summer a school-free zone, a two-month-long recess.

We stuck with the program, but without strong parental support, it was doomed, like the League of Nations without the United States. Having reason and justice on your side has never been enough.

Unless you also have the culture of the community on your side, you are bound to lose.

No one needs to tell me that life isn't like the movies, but just imagine if it were. All educational issues would be solvable, all teachers good-looking, and all students high achievers. School boards wouldn't be mired in trivia or discouraged by budget woes. Their meetings would be full of drama and excitement and still somehow be over—not including the closing credits—in a cool ninety minutes.

Chapter Four

Not with a Bang

I found out that the high school had quietly dropped social studies as a course for ninth graders on what had been, until then, a beautiful spring day.

My youngest daughter, who was in eighth grade, had brought home her ninth-grade schedule for me to sign. Even before I looked at it, as she was still in the process of handing it to me, I heard in the back of my head a premonitory "uh-oh." Having had three older children already pass through the district, I have acquired a kind of ESP about communications from school, and it is almost never wrong.

It wasn't wrong in this case either.

The schedule listed all the courses available to next year's ninth graders, with a check beside the ones Darla would be taking. I saw Math A, Earth Science, English, Phys. Ed., and something called Internet Research checked off, but no social studies listed anywhere on the paper. Ironically, social studies is Darla's favorite subject. She talks about being a social studies teacher when she grows up—that is, if she doesn't make it as an FBI agent/supermodel.

I pointed out the absence of social studies to Darla. "Yeah," she said, "I know. The guidance counselor explained it."

I wondered how anyone in the post–9/11 world could possibly explain not teaching fourteen- and fifteen-year-olds social studies for an entire year. It isn't like kids are well versed in history or geography or current events when they graduate from high school. The fact is, about 30 percent of them can't even find the Pacific Ocean on a map.

And that isn't all they can't find. According to a 2002 survey by *National Geographic*, the vast majority of eighteen- to twenty-four-year-olds also can't find Afghanistan or Iraq. Americans their own age are fighting and dying there, but they don't have a clue as to where "there" is. This seems a pretty serious deficiency in their education. As citizens of the world's greatest power, shouldn't they have a clearer picture of the world?

You would think so. But when my wife got the high school principal on the phone, he offered all kinds of rationales for why social studies was being dropped from the ninth-grade curriculum: no state law required that social studies be taught to ninth graders; the kids would be more developmentally ready to take Global Studies in tenth grade; other districts in the county dropped it first.

As she recounted the conversation to me at dinner, I was stunned by just how much things had changed in the year since I had lost my seat on the school board. The idea used to be to emulate the best practices of other districts. Was it now to emulate the worst?

Despite what the principal said, I knew from my experience on the board that the decision to drop ninth-grade social studies was largely money-driven. Faculty who had taught it would no doubt be shifted to the remedial social studies courses recently mandated by the state, eliminating the need for new hires. The annual school budget would still rise—like hot air, it always does—but not as high as it would have otherwise.

I could follow the current board's thinking; I just couldn't agree with it. One of the board members was the same man who had asked me when I was new to the board, "Do you people"—I'm Jewish—"celebrate Thanksgiving?" Anyone who has to ask that question after a certain age needs some remedial social studies himself. The board, in deciding it couldn't afford to pay for ninth graders to take social studies, was deciding it could afford to perpetuate his kind of ignorance among students.

What bothered me even more was that the teachers and administrators in the district didn't object to the decision. They just went along with it, like Germans after the Reichstag fire. Shouldn't they have murmured at least a few words of protest? Didn't they realize what they were saying by their silence? That only required subjects count. That social studies isn't important. That there is no harm in treating the rest of the world as if it were a boring TV show you can zap with the remote.

I never signed Darla's schedule. Instead, I scribbled a note on the bottom of it outlining my concerns. I also left voice mails for school board members and e-mailed the superintendent—twice. In one of the e-mails, I quoted a warning Thomas Jefferson had written in his old age: "If a nation expects to be ignorant and free in a state of civilization, it expects what never was and never will be."

This display of erudition must have violated district policy. Weeks passed, and neither the superintendent nor anyone else got back in touch with me.

But something did happen in the meantime, something awful. A boy who had gone to school with one of my sons died in a vehicle collision in Iraq. He was serving with the Army Reserve. He was twenty years old.

A couple hundred people crowded into the high school gym for a memorial service. The Army sent a major general to speak. "War isn't fair," the general said. "Freedom isn't free." He gave the dead boy's parents a folded American flag.

Just a few days later, the local paper ran a story about the Army denying the parents, who had emigrated from China in the 1960s and were desperately poor, thousands of dollars in benefits. The Army had ruled that their son's death wasn't combat-related.

When I finished reading the story, I felt angry and depressed, and it suddenly seemed to me that the way we educate our children exposes them not to knowledge or understanding, but to hate and fear and insane violence.

Flags were still flying at half-mast outside all the schools.

Chapter Five

Wilderness Road

In a public education system whose terminology is composed largely of misleading euphemisms and impenetrable jargon, the term "guidance office" may be the greatest misnomer of all. This isn't a knock on the work ethic of high school guidance counselors. I'm sure many important activities occur down at the guidance office. It is just that none of them qualify as guidance in any meaningful sense.

To guide, Webster's dictionary says, means to "lead or direct . . . in a course or path." It also means to "instruct and influence intellectually and morally; to train." Moreover, a guide is defined as, among other things, "one who . . . directs another in his conduct or course of life." By these definitions, guidance counselors aren't actually guides and what they do isn't actually guidance.

So what do they do?

A 2002 survey by the National Center for Education Statistics (NCES) found that guidance counselors spent the most time on course schedules and the second-most time on college applications. They spent the third-most time on attendance, discipline, and other school problems. Nowhere was there reference to time spent directing the intellectual and moral growth of students or serving as their friends and mentors.

The reason for this should be apparent—too many students and too few guidance counselors. According to the NCES survey, the nationwide ratio of public high school students to full-time guidance counselors is 315:1. In my local school district, the ratio is worse, a staggering 400:1. Given such numbers, it is impossible for guidance counselors to give close personal attention to each student. They are lucky if they can even match student faces with names.

But just because students don't get personal attention doesn't mean they don't need it. Young people are literally dying from a lack of adult guidance. One survey found that nearly three million Americans ages twelve to seventeen considered suicide in 2000, and that more than a third of them actually tried to kill themselves. "That is mayhem," said the executive director of San Francisco Suicide Prevention. "It means there is real chaos in homes and schools everywhere."

Under pressure from the federal No Child Left Behind Act, most schools today see their primary responsibility as raising test scores rather than caring for students. When William Glasser, founder of the Quality School Consortium, holds workshops, he interviews six junior or senior high school students in front of a large audience. He always asks the students, "Where in school do you feel important?" and they always look at him as if the question came from outer space. Feeling important simply isn't part of their experience of school.

Their predominant experience is that school is an unfriendly place where teasing and gossiping prevail and no one is willing to talk to you about your problems. Karin Oerlemans and Heather Jenkins, in a survey of high school students who were chronically absent, found that teachers and administrators aren't listening to students, and perhaps don't know how to listen to them. School, in effect, ignores the very people it should be nurturing.

Students who feel ignored—the clinical word for it is "alienated," lacking a sense of belonging—may do more than cut school. Psychologist Irwin Hyman of Temple University noted that one characteristic common to recent school shootings is that the shooters were alienated from their school cultures. Alienation has also been associated with academic failure, sexual promiscuity, and substance abuse. Faced with a restless, alienated student body, and the vast potential for disorder that implies, school officials tend to obsess on discipline. The rural high school my oldest daughter attends may not have a full complement of Advanced Placement courses, but it does have a half-dozen employees dedicated to monitoring and controlling student behavior. They include a school resource officer (that is, a cop), a behavior intervention specialist, a social worker, and a substance abuse counselor. In addition, the vice principal spends most of her time patrolling the halls for loiterers and the bathrooms for smokers when she could be spending it supporting classroom instruction.

Bigger schools come equipped with even more elaborate controls—metal detectors, surveillance cameras, walkie-talkies, drug-sniffing dogs—to keep students in check. The irony is that the police-state atmosphere does nothing to address the underlying causes of student alienation. If anything, it is yet another powerful reason for students to feel alienated. Educators talk all the time about putting "children first," but students know from daily experience that school policies and rules take precedence over their own needs and interests. They can't even walk down the hall or sit in the cafeteria without feeling harassed.

Remember the TV comedy *Cheers*? Its theme song described the friendly neighborhood tavern in which the show was set as a place where "everybody knows your name." William R. Capps and Mary Ellen Maxwell have suggested that school should be a place like that (though, presumably, without the bar stools). "Our children need to know school as a place where they feel a personal connection," Capps and Maxwell wrote in *American School Board Journal*, "a place where someone knows their dreams and fears, a place where they feel safe." The question is how to get there.

I can tell you it isn't by doing what we did when I was on the local school board. All of us had heard horror stories about the high school guidance program from parents—how students had been shunted into academic dead ends; how they had been told not to worry about taking advanced math, advanced science, a foreign language, or the SATs; how they had been advised to apply to colleges for which they were unqualified; how they had been allowed to daydream and drift. We were determined to fix that. First, we coaxed into retirement two guidance counselors who had been at the high school since it opened in the sixties, replacing them with younger, more vibrant counselors conversant with the latest theories on adolescent development. Second, we added another secretary to the guidance office to rescue the counselors from the sea of paperwork. Third, we remodeled the office to make it an appealing place for students to hang out. Fourth, we bought computer software specifically designed to help students with college and career planning. Then, tired but elated, we sat back to watch what would happen.

To our astonishment, nothing did. Guidance stayed the same sad mess it had always been. A thin layer of academically gifted students at the top continued to receive special attention, as did a somewhat thicker layer of academically challenged students at the bottom. But the vast majority of students, the students in the middle, those Powell, Farrar, and Cohen's classic study *The Shopping Mall High School* called "the unspecial," were still just "a great gray mass," and, as individuals, effectively written off.

I have only recently realized why our efforts miscarried. It was because we weren't bold enough in our thinking. We envisioned guidance in traditional terms, as confined to the guidance office, where the ratio of students to counselors remained hovering around 400:1. We really had no right, then, to expect the new counselors to do any better than the old counselors did. To give all students the kind of guidance they deserve would have required our adding about forty counselors, thereby reducing the student-counselor ratio to what it is at private schools, 10:1. My district, with its anorexic tax base, could never swallow such a thing, and probably neither can yours.

What we should have done was taken guidance out of the guidance office and given it to teachers. Colleges follow just this model. Professors, of which I'm one, are responsible for advising students as well as teaching them. I have fifteen to twenty student advisees every year. They are mine from the time they declare journalism as their major until they graduate. I do many of the typical tasks of a guidance counselor—approve their course schedules, write letters of recommendation, and so on. But because I see the students in class, and not merely during infrequent advising sessions, we have a relationship, a bond. They come to my office for more than my signature on forms. They come to bounce around ideas, borrow books, get reassurance, and sort out their feelings about college, journalism, the future.

Guidance of this kind doesn't require any special training. All it requires is a little friendly interest. And "between a teacher and a student," as Glasser pointed out, "a little friendly interest can go a long way." Mrs. Krevoruck, my ninth-grade English teacher, was the difference for me. I can still remember my happy embarrassment when she drew me aside one day after class and extravagantly praised a poem I had written for homework. It was like getting permission to become who I am.

"A system of education," Jerome Bruner said, "must help those growing up in a culture find an identity within that culture. Without it, they stumble in their effort after meaning." Every adolescent needs adult guidance, as the epidemic rates of teenage depression and suicide show, and teachers are the ones best situated to provide it. But, under the present system, relatively few teachers have the motivation to do so. High schools are filled with stumbling students, and school itself is often the biggest stumbling block.

Which leads me to a story about the great explorer and guide Daniel Boone, who blazed the Wilderness Road, the route used by thousands in the first westward migration. When Boone was an old man, someone asked him if he had ever been lost. He thought for a moment, then replied, "No, I was never lost, but I will admit to being bewildered for three days."

It is inevitable that adolescents, living through perhaps the most confusing stage of life, will occasionally feel bewildered. What isn't inevitable—what is, in fact, indefensible—is that they should ever feel lost and alone.

REFERENCES

Bruner, Jerome. *The Culture of Education*. Cambridge, Mass.: Harvard University Press, 1996.

Capps, William R., and Mary Ellen Maxwell. "Where Everybody Knows Your Name." *American School Board Journal*, September 1999.

Glasser, William. *The Quality School* (rev. ed.). New York: Harper, 1998.

Oerlemans, Karin, and Heather Jenkins. "Their Voice: Student Perceptions of the Sources of Alienation in Secondary School." Proceedings Western Australian Institute for Educational Research Forum 1998, http://education.curtin.edu.au/waier/forums/1998/oerlemans.html.

Powell, Arthur G., Eleanor Farrar, and David K. Cohen. *The Shopping Mall High School*. Boston: Houghton Mifflin, 1985.

Chapter Six

Graduation Day

As school board president, it was my duty for three years to sign the diplomas of graduating seniors. One year I also gave the commencement address, following my youngest son, the valedictorian of his class, to the podium. Only I knew just how ironic it was for me to sign diplomas, give a graduation speech, or father a valedictorian. Way back when, I had led a walkout from my own high school graduation.

Actually, "led" may be too strong a word. We were called up to receive our diplomas in alphabetical order. If my last name had begun with a letter later in the alphabet, an *S* or even a *K*, I wouldn't have been the first to walk out.

It was 1969. America's part in the Vietnam War had begun in earnest around the time my friends and I entered Merrick Avenue Junior High, and was still escalating as we prepared to graduate from John F. Kennedy High School. Growing up with the war had politicized us. We had heard the chants of "Hey, hey, LBJ, how many boys did you kill today?" We had seen the grisly photos in *Life* magazine of the My Lai massacre. We had learned that our government couldn't be trusted anymore to tell the truth.

Throughout high school, we had become increasingly impatient with our classes for lacking, in a catchword of the era, "relevance." It frustrated us that while the world smoked and crackled like a burning hooch, we sat in trigonometry class solving pointless problems or in English class parsing sample sentences. We wanted at least our graduation to be relevant, and so Neil, Dave, Andy, Steve, and I decided to wear black armbands to the ceremony as a protest against the war.

On graduation day some 500 seniors were lining up in the gym to march out to the football field when Mr. Witamak, a math teacher whose face always reminded me of a frog's, with bulgy eyes and wide, thin lips, began to shriek, "You can't wear that! You can't wear that!" He lunged at me and grabbed my armband and, after a moment's tussle, tore it off. Up and down the line, other teachers pounced on my friends.

We were shocked, outraged, humiliated—and at a loss about what to do next. But we knew we had to do something. The idea of a walkout took shape hurriedly, as we sweated on wooden folding chairs on the sun-scorched field, whispering back and forth across the rows.

"Should we do it?"

"I don't know. What do you think?"

"Let's do it."

"OK, we'll do it."

I would be the first of us called up to receive his diploma. By the time they got to the Gs, my heart was trying to crash through my chest. I scanned the bleachers for my family. There they were. I wondered how my parents would react. My mouth felt as if it were packed with a thousand cotton balls.

The whole thing was over quickly. I heard my name and walked up the steps and across the stage. The school board president smiled at me and extended his hand in congratulations. I didn't shake it, but thrust my arm high above my head and flashed the peace sign. Then I whirled on my heel and went down the steps. My friends rose from their chairs and marched off behind me to loud boos and scattered applause and with the hellish heat everywhere.

What happened after that is a blur to me, probably because of the adrenaline that was surging through my system, but I was later told fights broke out in the bleachers. One involved my grandpa Jake, a union organizer back in the thirties, with a broken nose twisted across his face to prove it. A family sitting nearby objected to his applauding us. Angry words were exchanged, and a few feeble punches thrown. Jake, who had seen a dozen grandchildren graduate from high school or college, would always say he never enjoyed a graduation more.

I'm tempted to end here, on the image of my grandpa, the happy warrior. But there is a coda to the story—or, if I stretch the timeline, three codas. Although I have often thought about it, I can't seem to decide which one provides the most appropriate moral.

Coda #1. The night of graduation, I was at a party, the Beatles' White Album playing on the stereo and couples making out in the corners. Someone came down the stairs and said the jocks were hunting all over town for my friends and me, promising to beat us up for ruining graduation. I began to tremble. Earlier in the day, I had found the courage to follow my conscience, but now I shook all over. I was afraid of being beaten up—I could picture a bunch of football players bashing in my face—and I was ashamed of being afraid.

Coda #2. A week before I went off to college, I stopped at the high school to retrieve my diploma. The vice principal, Mr. Rutledge, was in the office. He made a sadistic show of debating whether he should give me the diploma or not. When he finally handed it over, he said, "You'll regret what you did the rest of your life." Yeah, sure, I laughed to myself, but driving home in my mom's Buick, I kept worrying that his words might be some kind of Sophoclean curse. Had I committed an act of hubris by walking out, and would I pay for it, as the Greek heroes we had read about in AP English did, with mutilation and exile and wished-for death?

Coda #3. I bumped into Billy Roulette outside the door to the men's room at our twentieth high school reunion. A fellow runner on the cross-country team, he looked almost the same as he had when we used to pant up and down the hills of golf courses together. He shook my hand. "You were right," he said. I didn't know what he meant at first, and then I realized he meant Vietnam, graduation, the walkout.

To graduate implies moving from a lower stage of knowledge and experience to a higher one. Is that what happened to me on that long-ago day? All these years later, I'm still not sure. Did I show courage by walking out on graduation or reckless pride? Was I a hero for defying adult authority or a coward for dreading a possible beating? Or are there always a few of us, the fools and the pale, scrawny scholars, who graduate not from doubt to certainty, as most do, but from one agonizing doubt to another?

Chapter Seven

Honor Role

After the candle-lighting ceremony, during which old and new members of the local chapter had pledged to uphold the ideals of the National Honor Society (NHS), it was the adults' turn to speak. One after the other, the school board president, the high school principal, and the district superintendent marched on stage, mouthed a few polite words, then marched off. The superintendent, the most glib of the three, congratulated the honor society members for being outstanding students and us in the audience for being their parents. He said, "Give yourselves a round of applause," which we lustily did. Then everyone adjourned to the cafeteria for ice cream, punch, and photos.

But something bothered me about the evening, and a whole week passed before I finally realized what it was. None of the adults who spoke at the honor society induction had said anything about honor. Was this because honor is an archaic concept that went out with dueling pistols? Or was it because concepts go down easier when left vague and imprecise?

I didn't know. What I did know is that schools use the word "honor"—derived from the Latin *honos*, also the root of the word "honesty"—as if its meaning were self-evident. It isn't. Students qualify for honor roll and honor societies according to criteria that may actually have very little to do with honor as once practiced by trigger-happy cavaliers or now understood by moral philosophers.

Curious, I e-mailed the national office of NHS with a question: What is "honor"? I figured if anyone knew, an organization with the word in its name would. Within forty-eight hours, I got a reply, but not the one I had expected.

Associate director David Cordts wrote back that NHS doesn't have "a separate definition of honor." Instead, since its founding in 1921, it has used four criteria for selecting honor students: scholarship, leadership, service, and character. Cordts explained that NHS leaves "the actual details of the definitions of these terms to the local chapters." The chapter to which my oldest daughter, Brittany, belongs had defined scholarship as having a minimum average of 85, but this year abruptly raised the cutoff to 90. Perhaps someone had pointed out that, given rampant grade inflation, half the students in the school were now members, or at least eligible for membership.

Cordts invited me to post my question on the message board at NHS's website. I did—and got a grand total of one reply. It came from a chapter advisor who largely repeated what Cordts had already said. I began wondering whether the reason no one else shared their ideas of what "honor" meant was because they didn't have any ideas to share.

"Honor" has traditionally had two meanings, and NHS, though neither Cordts nor the chapter advisor seemed to realize it, reflects the most ancient of them. Like Aristotle, who described honor in his *Nicomachean Ethics* as "the prize of virtue and the tribute that we pay to the good," NHS views honor as closely related to public approbation. The advisor, for example, called membership in NHS "an honor for being honorable."

So perhaps the question I should have asked in my e-mail was "What does being honorable mean?" As best I can determine, it means following the rules, playing the game, striving to please authority. It means feeling that it is important, even necessary, to win the recognition and respect of others.

Aristotle believed that the impulse toward honor and the dread of dishonor were found only in the aristocratic class. "For it is the nature of the many," he wrote, "to be amenable to fear but not to a sense of honor, and to abstain from evil not because of its baseness but because of the penalties it entails." The typical high school operates as if it believes in a similar social hierarchy, sorting students by grade point average or athletic accomplishment into a relatively small group of nobles, a somewhat larger group of yeomen, and a teeming, faceless mass of peasants. If we want high school to operate differently—more, for example, democratically—then we must redefine what we mean by "honor."

There happens to be another definition available. "Honor" can also mean personal integrity, conscience. "It is possible," Curtis Brown Watson noted in *Shakespeare and the Renaissance Concept of Honor*, "that a man may paradoxically risk the loss of 'honor' (i.e., may fail to conform to the norms established by a given society which will win him the praise and esteem of his fellows) in order to preserve his 'honor' (i.e., avoid becoming dishonored in his own eyes)." "Honor," in this second sense, is often equated with "moral courage," a term that didn't appear in English until the nineteenth century.

Victorian philosopher Henry Sidgwick defined moral courage as people "facing the pains and dangers of social disapproval in the performance of what they believe to be duty." More recently, the Maine Commission on Ethical and Responsible Student Behavior said moral courage is doing "the right thing even if it's not popular." Moral courage is the courage of Socrates swallowing hemlock rather than drop his philosophical inquiries or repudiate his teachings. It is the courage of George Washington accepting appointment as commander-in-chief and then turning to Patrick Henry and saying, "Remember, Mr. Henry, what I now tell you: from the day I enter upon the command of the American armies, I date my fall, and the ruin of my reputation." It is the courage of a handful of non-Jews, the so-called "righteous gentiles," risking their lives and the lives of their families to shelter Jews from the Nazis during the Holocaust.

Courage has been described as an "executive virtue," meaning that it enables people to "execute," or carry out, their purposes. People who lack courage may be too fearful to act or, once embarked upon an action, too easily intimidated to finish it. For this reason, Samuel Johnson judged courage to be "the greatest of all virtues," explaining that "unless a man has that virtue, he has no security for preserving any other." Rushworth M. Kidder and Martha Bracy had something very similar in mind when they envisioned courage as "the hardware upon which the software of the other values operate."

If courage is, in fact, everything these writers say, then schools should be nurturing it in students. Movies and other forms of popular culture tend to spotlight physical courage, glamorizing ultra-violent acts of bloodshed inflicted out of rage or revenge. But democracy may not need muscle-bound warriors with hair-trigger tempers as much as it needs morally courageous citizens. After all, the average person is a lot more likely to have to fight insidious conformity than vampires, aliens, or the Russian mafia.

The difference between the two concepts of honor can be summed up as the difference between inner conviction and outer compulsion. When you picture the students on honor roll or in honor society, it probably isn't a bunch of cranky nonconformists you see, the kinds of kids who are always testing school rules or questioning teachers' authority. Probably you see the kinds of kids who quietly obey the rules and their teachers and save their ferocity for competing against each other for precious academic prizes—top grades, admission to AP courses, college scholarships. The students who succeed are those who can best accept external standards as their own.

This is apparent in the attitude of honor society members toward service, one of the four criteria for selection. Brittany's chapter requires members to perform at least twenty hours of community service each semester or be summarily expelled. They can fulfill the requirement in numerous ways, from serving as greeters at parent-teacher conference night to collecting canned food for needy families. It doesn't matter to most of them what they do, just as long as they accumulate hours. In other words, they aren't interested in service; they are interested in getting their hours done. I'm afraid that if the service requirement teaches them anything, it teaches them how to appear caring without actually being so.

To help students understand honor as an inner quality, a matter of individual courage or conscience, would seem to call for a different approach. One night Brittany complained at dinner that the vice principal at the high school was stopping girls in the hall and measuring the length of their skirts. Doesn't she have anything better to do? Brittany asked. Good question! My wife and I told her that if she felt so strongly about the injustice of the dress code, then she ought to do something about it. Like what? Brittany wanted to know. Like drawing up a petition. Or—my wife and I said it almost simultaneously—wearing a skirt (Brittany usually wears jeans, tight ones, to school) as a kind of political statement. Some of you may think that this last suggestion was irresponsible of us, that we must be the worst parents since Ma Barker to encourage our daughter to provoke a confrontation with school officials. But, in her world, the dress code is a big issue, bigger even than the war in Iraq, and we were trying to teach her not to ignore the promptings of her conscience. Courage is like a muscle; it gets stronger with use.

A couple days later, Brittany did wear a skirt, but the only ones who may have been agitated by it were the boys in her classes. The vice principal never checked her for a possible dress-code violation. Brittany came home from school feeling emboldened. She had discovered her capacity to challenge rules, not just follow them.

It is this capacity that constitutes honor in the most modern and meaningful sense. "Honor" as the prickly pride of the duelist belongs to another era, another culture. But perhaps no more so than the version of honor reflected in honor rolls and honor societies—honor as an example of, and a reward for, approved school behavior. NHS describes its members as "role models for other students."

What exactly, though, are they modeling? Is it scholarship? Leadership? Service? Character? Or is it something else, such as the material benefits of submitting, mind and body, to convention?

Honor isn't conformity to popular opinion. Rather, it is the courage to stand up to popular opinion. Honor isn't obedience to authority. Rather, it is the courage to question authority. Every teacher should know this, and every school should teach it. There is no honor in doing anything less.

REFERENCES

Kidder, Rushworth M., and Martha Bracy. "Moral Courage: A White Paper," www.globalethics.org.

Miller, William Ian. *The Mystery of Courage*. Cambridge, Mass.: Harvard University Press, 2000.

Watson, Curtis Brown. *Shakespeare and the Renaissance Concept of Honor*. Princeton, N.J.: Princeton University Press, 1960.

Chapter Eight

A Darkness Darker Than Night

"You should call the school, Dad," my daughter Darla said first thing off the bus.

A girl in her eighth-grade art class had drawn a swastika on the board during "free activity period"—another name, apparently, for Kristallnacht. The teacher didn't notice the swastika until Darla, one of the two Jewish students in the school, pointed it out to her.

I could remember my own collision with anti-Semitism back in junior high. We were playing softball in gym when I stroked a pitch into the gap. It was a triple for sure and maybe even a home run. But as I tore past the shortstop, he grumbled, "Dirty Jew." I sprung at him. He went down. I sat on his chest and pounded him in the face again and again and again.

The gym teacher, Mr. Mousehart, finally pulled me off.

"Are you crazy?" he screamed.

"He called me a 'dirty Jew.'"

Mr. Mousehart seized the shortstop by the scruff of the neck and dragged him away—if lucky, to the principal's office, and if not, to the locker room for a paddling.

The art teacher had merely taken the Hitler youth aside and huddled with her for a few moments. It was Darla who, upset at the teacher's low-key response, had marched down to the office after class to report the incident.

I played phone tag with the dean, the person in charge of student discipline, for a couple days. By the time I got him, he had spoken to the art teacher, who had told him that the girl didn't know she had drawn a swastika.

"You mean she saw it on a flag hanging on the wall at home, but didn't know what it was?" I asked.

He ignored my sarcasm. "She said she just likes the way it looks. She said it looks cool."

I was afraid the dean was going to launch into the kind of discussion you can find online about the swastika—how it was more than 3,000 years old, older even than the Egyptian ankh; how it showed up on pottery and coins from ancient Troy; how it was used by many cultures, including the Navajo, to represent life, sun, power, strength, and good luck.

All of which may be true, but once the swastika became the official symbol of the Nazi Party in 1920, it forever stopped being a good luck sign, especially for Jews.

"Listen," I said, "the swastika represents mass murder, the Final Solution. It's a traumatic symbol to someone who's Jewish."

I thought of my mother's mother, my grandma Blooma. She still had family in Poland when the Nazis invaded. After the war, she began a decade-long search for them. She contacted government agencies, Jewish organizations, the Red Cross. Nothing. It was as if her parents, sisters, brothers, aunts, uncles, and cousins had never existed. They had been swallowed by a darkness darker than night.

I told this story to the dean, but he seemed unmoved. "She didn't know it was a swastika," he merely repeated.

Maybe I shouldn't have been surprised that I was having such a hard time getting him to grasp the seriousness of what had happened in art class. People in his position—and principals, vice principals, and the like—tend to be better at deflecting problems than solving them. Besides, he was white and Christian in an overwhelmingly white and Christian community. He didn't know how it felt to be derided for your race or religion.

But my kids knew. As bad as the swastika on the board was, the casual anti-Semitism they have suffered year in and year out at school may be worse. They have endured insensitive questions ("How come you don't look Jewish?"). They have overheard racial slurs ("jew 'em down"). And whenever they have objected, they have received lame excuses ("Hey, I was only joking!").

These kinds of things happen despite the fact that the high school has a Diversity Club and the middle school a character education program. Students are encouraged at award assemblies, during morning announcements over the PA, and by colorful banners in the halls to show tolerance and respect for others—but all, predictably, with very limited results. According to a vast and growing body of research, unless the adults around them model a desired behavior, kids aren't likely to learn it, no matter how loudly or often you say they should.

I hung up from the dean feeling the rage and frustration Darla must have felt. There is something defective in the moral circuitry of a system that would send a student to the office for pushing in the cafeteria line, but not for drawing a swastika on the board.

Elie Wiesel, the Nobel laureate and Nazi concentration camp survivor, once remarked, "The opposite of love isn't hate, but indifference." It is sad that children are hated and ridiculed for being black or brown or gay or Jewish. It is even sadder that some internalize the hate. But the saddest thing of all must be that no one really gives a crap.

Chapter Nine

Schoolhouse Rock

When rock 'n' roll became the chosen music of American teenagers in the 1950s, adults got all shook up. A. M. Merrio, an associate professor of psychiatry at Columbia University, warned with a hysteria that rendered him nearly incoherent, "If we cannot stem the tide of rock and roll with its waves of rhythmic narcosis and future waves of vicarious craze, we are preparing our downfall in the midst of pandemic funeral dances." The Catholic Youth Center of Minneapolis urged kids to smash the rock 'n' roll records they owned. Bridgeport and New Haven, Connecticut, among other cities, banned rock concerts. A congressional subcommittee held hearings on the supposed link between rock music and juvenile delinquency.

The ability of rock 'n' roll to horrify adults only increased its appeal for teenagers, who adopted the music as a way of asserting generational identity. Rock's popularity among the young crystallized with the 1955 movie *Blackboard Jungle*, about a teacher's problems in dealing with juvenile delinquents at an inner-city school. The opening shot of the movie showed kids in a schoolyard surrounded by a high chain-link fence—a symbolic prison—while Bill Haley's "Rock around the Clock" boomed on the soundtrack. For teenagers across the country, the song became a call to break out of their "prison," to rise up and defy parents and teachers. For parents and teachers, it became another reason to hate rock 'n' roll.

Rock was the first form of music to exclusively cater to teenagers and their particular interests. Hard-rocking songs have been recorded about cars, sex, drugs, clothes, and even school. From its beginning, rock has provided an outlet for many of the negative feelings about school that young people haven't been allowed to express elsewhere.

I thought it might be both fun and useful to examine how some of the greatest rockers ever—Chuck Berry, the Ramones, Bruce Springsteen—have described school in their songs. Just don't be surprised that they often describe it as uneducational.

1. Ring, ring goes the bell / The cook in the lunch room's ready to sell / You're lucky if you can find a seat / You're fortunate if you have time to eat / Back in the classroom, open your books / Keep up the teacher don't know how mean she looks

Chuck Berry's "School Day," which reached number eight on the pop chart in 1957, portrays school as no place you would want to be. Directly addressing its teenage audience, the song reminds them that school is a dictatorship of clocks and bells, a rigid, relentless routine that refuses to bend to their hopes or needs. The adults mentioned in the song—the cook, the teacher—serve the system, not the students. More than a decade later, Charles E. Silberman, in his *Crisis in the Classroom*, would make the same point, though less succinctly: "Because adults take the schools so for granted, they fail to appreciate what grim, joyless places most American schools are, how oppressive and petty are the rules by which they are governed, how intellectually sterile and esthetically barren, what an appalling lack of civility obtains on the part of teachers and principals, what contempt they unconsciously display for children as children."

In the final verses of "School Day," Berry contrasts the dreariness of school with the freedom of rock 'n' roll. The lyrics carry listeners down the hall and into the street and around the corner to a "juke joint," where music and dancing provide emotional release. Berry hails rock 'n' roll for saving the young from being smothered in drudgery, for delivering them from "the days of old"—in effect, the boring adults who run schools for their own convenience rather than for the good of kids.

2. *Well, we busted out of class / Had to get away from those fools / We learned more from a three-minute record, baby / Than we ever learned in school*

Bruce Springsteen's "No Surrender," from his enormously popular 1984 album, *Born in the U.S.A.*, begins where Berry's song ends, with students slipping out through the prison bars of school. But Springsteen doesn't portray rock 'n' roll as simply a form of escape; he proposes it as a kind of alternative education. Progressive educators have been suggesting something similar for more than a century. "From the standpoint of the child," John Dewey wrote in *My Pedagogic Creed* (1897), "the great waste in the school comes from his inability to utilize the experiences he gets outside the school in any complete and free way within school itself." Rather than school officials censoring youth culture—their usual policy—perhaps they should treat it as a resource.

Messing around on the Internet or obsessively watching the *Godfather* movies may not seem like worthwhile endeavors, but virtually any teenage activity or interest can be a starting point for further learning. To take just one example, I know a boy whose interest in muscle cars became, with the right encouragement, the inspiration to study chemical engineering. The "fools" in Springsteen's song are teachers who don't get this, who don't realize that interests are what Dewey called "the signs and symptoms of growing power." School will inevitably have the feel of prison, dismal and repressive, for teenagers as long as it continues to isolate them from the most interesting parts of their lives.

3. *When I think back / On all the crap I learned in high school / It's a wonder I can think at all*

Paul Simon criticizes school in his sardonic "Kodachrome," off the 1973 album, *There Goes Rhymin' Simon*, not for being boring or irrelevant, but for being downright harmful. And he isn't the only rocker to feel this way. The Ramones, considered by many the first bona fide punk rock band, sing to the deceptively cheerful beat of "Rock 'n' Roll High School" (1979), "I hate the teachers and the principal / Don't wanna be taught to be no fool." About twenty years later, the alternative metal band Rage Against the Machine shrieked much the same message in "Take the Power Back": "The teacher stands in front of the class / But the lesson plan he can't recall / The students' eyes don't perceive the lies / Bouncing off every fucking wall."

These songs—and several others, including Pink Floyd's "Another Brick in the Wall Part 2" ("We don't need no education / We don't need no thought control")—envision teachers as pouring information into students' heads like wet cement, which, once dry, leaves their brains immobilized. Some of the songs hint that this happens by malignant design, others that it happens through carelessness or inadvertence. All agree, though, as to what the ultimate effect is: students can't think, or if they can think, it isn't their own thoughts they are thinking, but those of the political and social establishment.

Long before the invention of rock 'n' roll, writers and philosophers were already expressing dismay that most teachers approach students as just so many boxes to be filled. In 1929, when the hot new dance was the turkey trot, Alfred North Whitehead warned against the teaching of "inert ideas"—"ideas that are merely received into the mind without being utilized, or tested, or thrown into fresh combinations." He pointed out, as Immanuel Kant had pointed out earlier and Jerome Bruner and other school reformers have pointed out since, that "the valuable intellectual development is self-development." "Let the main ideas which are introduced into a child's education be few and important . . . . ," Whitehead said. "The child should make them his own, and should understand their application here and now in the circumstances of his actual life."

Educational policymakers paid about as much attention to Whitehead's advice as they would to the comments and criticisms of long-haired, coke-snorting rockers. Under the latest government guidelines, the central purpose of education isn't to free the young to think for themselves, but to test them whenever possible. If kids are learning anything in school today, it is to binge and purge—to cram madly for tests, then regurgitate the information like a bunch of bulimics.

4. *Back to school and I hate it there, I hate it there / Everything I want I gotta wait a year, I wait a year / This nigga graduated at the top of my class / I went to Cheesecake, he was a motherfucking waiter there*

To the old complaint that school is useless and boring, rapper Kanye West adds in "School Spirit," from his 2004 album, *The College Dropout*, that it is also racist. I glimpsed just how racist while attending the induction ceremony for National Junior Honor Society at my daughter Darla's middle school. Despite the rising enrollment of black students throughout the district, there weren't any blacks among either the inductees or the inductors. Almost as disturbing, no one remarked on their absence. It was as if white were the expected color of academic achievement.

Journalist Meredith Maran found a similar imbalance during a year she spent investigating life at Berkeley (Calif.) High School, one of the top public high schools in the country—if you happen to be white. Most of the school's white students "graduate and go off to four-year colleges," she noted, but most of its black and Latino students "drop out, flunk out, or go off to junior college, low-wage jobs, or jail." The National Task Force on Minority Achievement exposed some of the roots of this kind of hopelessness and failure when it reported in 1999 that only 17 percent of black and 24 percent of Latino high school seniors were proficient in reading, and that only 4 percent of blacks were proficient in math and science.

Blacks tend to underachieve in school not because they are inferior, but because their backgrounds often are. They are born into poor families and grow up in murderous neighborhoods and go to crumbling schools where they are taught by the worst teachers. Kids of any color who grew up as too many black kids do, battered by racism and adrift in poverty, would suffer the same educational blight, the same sense of defeat, the same exhausted futures.

"The most deadly of all possible sins," Montessori teacher-turned-psychoanalyst Erik Erikson said, "is the mutilation of a child's spirit." For half a century, all kinds of rockers have protested the gruesome mutilations and maimings inflicted on children at school. But as popular with teenagers as this music has been, it hasn't actually improved the state of American public education. Students still must sit through boring classes and abide by oppressive rules. Which is why, if you listen closely to your kids when they talk about school, you may hear the words and music of new songs forming.

REFERENCES

Dewey, John. "My Pedagogic Creed" in *Dewey on Education*, ed. Martin S. Dworkin. New York: Teachers College Press, 1959.

Maran, Meredith. *Class Dismissed*. New York: St. Martin's Press, 2000.

Martin, Linda. *Anti-Rock: The Opposition to Rock 'n' Roll*. Hamden, Conn.: Archon Books, 1988.

Silberman, Charles E. *Crisis in the Classroom*. New York: Random House, 1970.

Whitehead, A. N. *The Aims of Education and Other Essays*. New York: Macmillan, 1929.

Chapter Ten

Straight to Hell

What is the difference between heaven and hell?

In hell, people sit at a long, food-filled table with their arms chained. The chains are loose enough that they can reach out for the delicious food, but tight enough that they can't bring the food to their mouths.

Heaven presents the same situation. The same banquet table. The same chains. But in heaven, people have the sense to realize that they can raise their arms high enough to feed the person next to them. People help each other, and it is a perpetual feast.

I was reminded of this Hasidic parable by the ugliness that surrounded the creation of the latest school budget. As the school board wrestled with the numbers—and kept getting body-slammed—the community grew increasingly uneasy. There were rumors that the board was going to eliminate a couple of vice principals, some teachers, more teacher aides, JV cheerleading, AP classes, and full-day kindergarten. Even if only a fraction of the rumors were true, the district risked being plunged into chaos and mournful wailing, somewhat like Iraq after the United States "liberated" it.

"Everything's on the table," one board member confirmed when I called her. I heard the same exact phrase from another member I phoned. It was obviously the board's budget mantra. I had a vision of board members holding hands in executive session and chanting in unison, "Everything's on the table, everything's on the table, everything's . . ."

Paradoxically, despite all the stuff on the table, there was a sudden danger of malnutrition. The board wasn't focused so much on keeping students educationally fed as on limiting the cost of feeding them. If an AP class had fewer than fifteen students enrolled, the board wanted to take it off the table and shove it down the disposal. If a club or sports team had fewer than twelve members, the board wanted to shove that down, too. I feared that with these kinds of things dropped from the school menu, kids would suffer from shocking deficiencies in their diet, the educational equivalent of rickets or beriberi.

Others might have felt similarly but were too busy competing for board funding to recognize it. At public meetings and behind the scenes, the moms of kindergartners vied with the moms of cheerleaders, middle school administrators with high school ones, teachers with teacher aides. The board had re-created, in the heat of drafting a budget, the greedy, selfish conditions of what the parable described as hell.

How did it happen? It wasn't because board members are, as some suspect, the spawn of Satan. Rather, it was because the board made saving money, not providing a good education, the point of the budget process.

A school budget is more than a financial document. First and foremost, it is a kind of manifesto, a declaration to the world of a board's educational philosophy and aims. When board members told me, "Everything's on the table," they were basically saying they had no philosophy, or at least no more than that of a clerk adding up cash register receipts at the end of his shift at 7-Eleven.

"What the best and wisest parent wants for his own child," John Dewey once wrote, "that must the community want for all its children." A board that begrudges spending money on kindergarten or AP classes isn't acting like the best and wisest parent. It is acting more like the evil stepmother in a fairy tale.

It is also acting as if it were afraid of provoking the community's wrath. Every year of the six years I served on the school board, we would nervously try to guess just how much we could propose raising taxes—2 percent? 5 percent? 8 percent?—and still be allowed to live in the community. The irony is that few people ever appreciated our efforts. I can still remember a man, his face red with anger, jumping up at a board meeting and bitterly accusing us of extravagance—of having, he sputtered, "champagne tastes on beer money."

This was the same meeting where we decided we couldn't afford new social studies textbooks, even though those used by seventh graders contained a map of the former Soviet Union labeled USSR. One day my daughter Darla, looking down at the map, had asked me what USSR meant. "It means," I had said, "your book is out of date."

Budget time was always the worst time of the year for me. I never felt more exposed to the crush of forces beyond my control. At least 90 percent of the budget was consumed by fixed costs, everything from state-mandated programs and services to fuel for buses to interest on debt. Arguing over how to divide up the rest—the main activity of the board during budget time—was a bit ludicrous, like arguing over the change on your dresser.

As put to voters, the latest school budget kept full-day kindergarten and most AP classes, but cut administrators, teachers, teacher aides, and JV cheerleading. It passed, to the board's giddy relief, by 34 votes. Then again, only 972 of the 8,000-plus eligible voters in the district actually voted.

Maybe if the board had expressed in the budget a clearer vision of educational excellence, more voters would have been inspired to turn out. But maybe not. Maybe despite the table being heaped with food, we are doomed by our own shortsightedness and cupidity to go hungry.

Chapter Eleven

The Deepest Cut

Only a school board that badly needs board training would ever do what my local school board has done—cut the miniscule portion of the district's budget that paid for board training. It is the kind of paradox that, pondered too long, can cause your head to hemorrhage. So I guess I'd better make this quick.

Board members justified the cut by pointing to the tough economic climate. But how does cutting $8,000 from a $30 million budget help cope with that? Isn't it a lot like trying to lose weight by trimming your toenails?

The truth is, the board members cut the funding for training because they felt they already knew everything worth knowing about serving on a school board. They don't, and neither do many other board members around the country. A 2004 survey of school officials in Pennsylvania found that respect, open-mindedness, and teamwork should be the top characteristics of board members. It also found that the typical board member, particularly when first elected, is close-minded, lacks knowledge of major issues, and gets into frequent screaming matches.

None of us learns to drive by trial and error. Imagine the cost in wrecked cars and injured and killed if we did. Why should board members, who are steering a school district, something much more complex and unwieldy than a car, expect to do so without any training? We pay for their arrogance with widespread carnage—botched programs, misguided policies, neglected students.

According to the latest count by the National School Boards Association, sixteen states mandate training for board members, and another ten have some form of certification. Requirements vary. New Jersey, Arkansas, and Missouri require training for newly elected members only. Georgia requires twelve hours of training annually for new members and six hours for all other members. Texas requires the entire board to participate annually with their superintendent in a team-building session of at least three hours.

In most states that mandate training, the state school boards association provides the bulk of it. Topics include education law, education finance, conflict management, board responsibilities, and the board–superintendent relationship. The last is notoriously volatile, not unlike the relationship between the black widow and her mate, though, in this instance, it is the community that usually gets screwed and devoured.

Support for mandatory training may be growing. Recently, blue-ribbon panels in both Pennsylvania and New York endorsed the concept. Those who favor mandatory training argue that higher standards for students, as required by the federal No Child Left Behind Act, require higher standards for board members as well. "There is no doubt," Tim Kremer, executive director of the New York State School Board Association, said, "that higher quality of student achievement in a school district is related to the quality of governance in that district."

But there is no doubt either that some school boards prefer doing their job as they deem fit, and not as the experts tell them they should. Kremer himself admitted that just raising the possibility of mandatory board training would be "controversial" to the members of his group. It is a strange attitude for people entrusted with overseeing our public schools. I mean, doesn't it kind of contradict the whole idea behind education?

That, in the end, is what disturbs me the most. When I consider my school board's decision to cut the money for board training out of the budget, I'm struck by the smugness involved in it, the implied disdain for continued learning. If teachers or administrators exhibited similar disdain, they would deserve to be fired. And if students did, they would deserve to flunk.

Board members who want students to become lifelong learners must model lifelong learning themselves. Board members who want teachers and administrators to continually update their knowledge and skills must continually update their own. The spirit of a school district is in the keeping of its board members and flows out from them to others, sometimes as light, sometimes as warmth, and sometimes, like now, as darkness.

REFERENCES

Elizabeth, Jane. "School Board Reform Elusive." *Pittsburgh Post-Gazette* (December 1, 2003), http://www.post-gazette.com.

———. "School Board's Worth in Doubt." *Pittsburgh Post-Gazette* (November 30, 2003), http://www.post-gazette.com.

Howell, William G. "School Boards Besieged." *Education Week* (March 9, 2005): 32, 44.

Chapter Twelve

The Bard of Education

I was sifting through the jumble of books on the remainder table, as I always do at bookstores, when I spotted among the former best-sellers, out-of-date almanacs, and quickie celebrity biographies a handsome hardcover translation of Heracleitus's *Fragments*. Heracleitus, who lived in the Greek city of Ephesus 2,500 years ago, is famous for having said you can never step into the same river twice. Other poetic aphorisms of his, while perhaps less well known, are no less wise.

When I got the book home—it only cost me $4.99, about the price of renting a new release from Blockbuster—and began to read it, I was immediately struck by its potential relevance for school board members (and without being due back before noon two days hence).

Because a copy of *Fragments* may not be lying buried under the diet books on the remainder table at your nearest bookstore, I have chosen a few sayings by Heracleitus to discuss in relation to school board membership. If turning for guidance to an ancient Greek with a one-word name seems odd to you, I would point out that Sting also has a one-word name and he is a rock star. Besides, school board members, saddled with an often impossible job, need all the wisdom they can borrow.

So what exactly does Heracleitus have to say?

1. Men dig tons of earth to find an ounce of gold. As applied to school boards, this means that boards can expend enormous time and effort on some question or goal and still accomplish very little of substance.

I have listened to board members—and, unfortunately, you may have, too—debate for hours the relative costs of various types of outdoor fencing, as if it were an important educational issue. They would probably say in their own defense that they were only trying to protect local taxpayers. Actually, the best way to protect taxpayers isn't to spend almost an entire board meeting arguing which is more cost-effective, plastic or steel mesh, but to ensure that teachers and administrators are doing what they are paid to do—create schools that are imaginative, nurturing, and vibrant.

2. *Whoever cannot seek the unforeseen sees nothing, for the known way is an impasse.* School boards that followed this advice would be willing to take risks. They wouldn't be bound by habit or tradition. They would be experimenters, innovators, trendsetters. Too often the educational establishment (which, like it or not, includes most school boards) resists serious change, clinging to the familiar for political and psychological safety.

You can see this in how states and the federal government have gone about trying to raise academic standards in the past decade. Did the various education departments encourage new styles of pedagogy? Hardly. Did they develop new forms of assessment? I don't think so. Did they invite student input? Absolutely not. Their approach was simply to order schools to do something they already did—test students, only to do it earlier, harder, and in more subjects.

In New York, one of the first states to expand annual high-stakes testing, the results have been impressive: record numbers of students dropping out, record numbers in danger of not graduating from high school on schedule, record numbers overtested and undereducated (if being educated means having an active, curious mind). These aren't the results anyone intended, but what else was possible when the kind of schooling that caused a crisis in student achievement in the first place was enlisted to solve that crisis?

Heracleitus was right: you can't get to a new destination by taking the same old, rutted road.

3. *Seekers of wisdom first need sound intelligence.* A school board's decisions on everything from budget to curriculum to personnel can be no better than the information on which the decisions are based. Or, as Heracleitus himself puts it in another fragment, "Let's not make rash guesses our most lucid thoughts."

Board members should listen at least as much as they talk—and probably more. They should, of course, evaluate what the superintendent and other administrators say, but should generally be able to trust it, and if they can't, they should hire people whose words they can trust. They should also consult teachers, parents, and students when feasible. With this caution: not everyone is equally competent to offer advice on every issue.

My local school board recently surveyed parents of high schoolers about block scheduling, which has been a source of controversy in the district ever since it went into effect in the late 1990s. The survey asked, among other things, what subjects should be taught in the block and why. Although parents may have strong opinions on this, most aren't qualified by work or training to informatively discuss it, and basing educational policy on their responses might well be a fiasco, like determining the solutions to math problems by popular vote.

School boards should ask parents for their ideas and recommendations, but about matters in which they have expertise. A big part of gathering sound intelligence is knowing who is equipped to answer which questions.

4. *Dogs . . . bark at what they cannot understand.* If some board members weren't lecturing their colleagues or berating school employees, they wouldn't have much to do. Many boards are burdened with at least one member who should probably seek immediate psychiatric help, who lives in a thick, dark haze of ignorance, anger, and suspicion.

These are the members who will pervert any topic or occasion into an opportunity to verbally stomp someone, whether unionized teachers or losing coaches or liberal parents. And whatever they say, they are sure to say it in a way that would make even a notorious loudmouth like George Steinbrenner cringe.

I once heard a board member tell a principal in executive session to grow a pair of . . . you know. I have heard other board members be nearly as insulting in public. They don't seem to understand the difference between holding an employee accountable and holding him or her hostage. School boards will never receive genuine respect, or deserve it, while there are members who snarl and snap like ill-tempered dogs and need to be followed around with a pooper-scooper.

5. *The cosmos works by harmony of tensions, like the lyre and the bow.* A school board is made up of distinct individuals who, if they are ever going to get anything done together, must submerge their individuality. Board members either learn to reconcile their differences or waste their time in office flailing about in chaos and contention.

Another thing board members would do well to learn is how to cope with ambiguity. Heracleitus implied as much when he said, "The beginning is the end." That is, good/bad, yea/nay, problem/solution exist as separate categories only in our heads. In reality, the boundaries between the up and down sides of a decision are neither clear nor fixed.

For example, a board may, after long, anguished deliberation, finally approve a policy permitting out-of-state field trips, but within days, the eruption of terrorist attacks, government alerts, and scare headlines may beset the policy with migraine-inducing complications the board had no way of foreseeing. Board members would shorten their meetings and perhaps extend their lives by recognizing and accepting that they can't control everything that happens.

Such a mental adjustment isn't easy, especially for the kind of willful, opinionated people who often run for the school board. They tend to believe they have discovered the one sure cure for what ails public education; that is precisely why they run. It is also why many end up frustrated and bitter and looking for someone, anyone—the superintendent, teachers, other board members—to blame when things don't work out quite as they envisioned.

Heracleitus belongs to the tradition of wisdom poetry that in the East includes Lao-tzu and Confucius, and in the West the Old Testament books of Proverbs, Job, and Ecclesiastes. It may seem ludicrous to recommend the writings of an ancient Greek philosopher-poet to board members embroiled in the tedious details of budget-making or personnel evaluation. Then again, I don't know any school board that wouldn't benefit from a touch of poetry. Do you?

Chapter Thirteen

These Truths

For their final number at the spring concert, the middle school chorus sang a rousing rendition of Lee Greenwood's red-blooded, flag-waving "I'm Proud to Be an American." The song may give others goose bumps, but it gives me the beginnings of a migraine.

Don't get me wrong. I'm proud to be an American, too . . . most of the time. But I found it unsettling to hear a couple dozen teeny-boppers—including my daughter Darla—singing lustily about God and country and war. I felt a little like I was attending a pep rally for the Joint Chiefs of Staff.

I mentioned this to my wife, Barbara, as we were leaving the concert. "Do they have to sing that crap? It's a song for rednecks and incipient fascists. Why can't they sing something that sticks it to authority?" I was thinking of Pete Seeger's "Where Have All the Flowers Gone?" or Bob Dylan's "Blowin' in the Wind."

Barbara gave me a pitying look. "Because people don't want to stick it to authority," she said.

Oh.

My wife's analysis is no doubt correct, but that doesn't mean worship of power and authority is. Educators in a democracy have a responsibility to kindle in their students what Thomas Jefferson called "the sacred fire of freedom and self-government."

The best way to do that isn't by singing patriotic hymns. Nor is it by sending, as Darla's health class did, holiday greetings to the sailors aboard the USS *Abraham Lincoln*, a nuclear-powered aircraft carrier patrolling the Persian Gulf. Of course, there is nothing really wrong with these activities, but there is nothing really democratic about them either. They would be just as welcome in a dictatorship as in a democracy.

No, the best way to light the fire may be by infusing the curriculum with the values of the nation's founding document, the Declaration of Independence, particularly its second paragraph: "We hold these Truths to be self-evident, that all Men are created equal, that they are endowed by their Creator with certain unalienable Rights, that among these are Life, Liberty, and the Pursuit of Happiness." Abraham Lincoln—the sixteenth president, not the aircraft carrier—once referred to this statement as "the father of all moral principles."

The Declaration isn't the only sacred American text. We also have, for example, the Constitution and the Bill of Rights. But only the Declaration rings with assertions about men's original equality, or their unalienable rights, or the sovereignty of the people. As historian Vernon Parrington pointed out, "The humanitarian idealism of the Declaration has always echoed a battle-cry in the hearts of those who dream of an America dedicated to democratic ends." During the past 200 years, farmers, laborers, abolitionists, suffragettes, and other embattled groups have enlisted its principles on behalf of their struggles for equality.

It is this capacity of the Declaration to convince and inspire that Lincoln particularly cherished. When he challenged Stephen A. Douglas, the "Little Giant," for the Senate in 1858, the Declaration provided one of the running themes of their famous debates.

Douglas claimed that the equality clause and the guarantees of life, liberty, and the pursuit of happiness applied only to whites. "I am not only opposed to negro equality," he announced, "but I am opposed to Indian equality. I am opposed to putting the coolies, now importing into this country, on equality to us."

But Lincoln argued that the Declaration made no distinctions based on birth or race. The signers, he said, "meant to set up a standard maxim for free men which should be familiar to all, and revered by all; instantly looked to, and constantly labored for, and even though never perfectly attained, constantly approximated and thereby instantly spreading and deepening its influence, and augmenting the happiness and values of life to all people of all colors everywhere." According to a contemporary transcript, the audience responded to his words with "loud and long continued applause."

The Declaration is significant today, as it already was in Lincoln's day, less as a statement of why the colonies separated from Britain than as a rule for living. Carl Becker, one of the foremost historians of the Declaration, wrote movingly of what it has asked of generations of Americans: "At its best, it preached toleration in place of persecution, goodwill in place of hate, peace in place of war. It taught that beneath all local and temporary diversity . . . all men are equal in the possession of a common humanity: and to the end that concord might prevail on the earth instead of strife, it invited men to promote in themselves the humanity which bound them to their fellows and to shape their conduct and their institutions in harmony with it."

That we are still embroiled in miserable wars, still fouling the earth with hate and injustice, shouldn't be blamed on some fundamental flaw in the Declaration, but on the feebleness of our effort to live up to its implicit demands.

Rep. Roger Wicker recently visited the Advanced Placement history class at a high school in his Mississippi congressional district. When he asked the students to name some of the unalienable rights listed in the Declaration, he got silence. So he gave them a hint. "Among these are life," he said, "and . . ."

"Death?" one student ventured.

The results are just as dismal at lower grades. Twenty-five percent of the fourth graders who took the National Assessment of Educational Progress in U.S. history in 2001 didn't know that the Fourth of July celebrates the Declaration. They thought it marked the end of the Civil War, the start of women's right to vote, or the arrival of the Pilgrims.

Education has always been entrusted with the task of molding the young into responsible citizens, though how well the task has been carried out and what constitutes responsible citizenship have differed from culture to culture and age to age. Amid the gloomy threats of our own age—war, terrorism, pollution, poverty—the Declaration can help students, if its incandescent message is implanted in their hearts, to burn bright with Jefferson's sacred fire. Then oh say can you see them respect not only authority, but also principle; love not only their country, but also the planet; embrace not only their own kind, but also humankind.

REFERENCES

Becker, Carl. *The Declaration of Independence: A Study in the History of Ideas*. New York: Vintage Books, 1922.

Hawke, David. *A Transaction of Free Men: The Birth and Course of the Declaration of Independence*. New York: Charles Scribner's Sons, 1964.

Maeir, Pauline. *American Scripture: Making the Declaration of Independence*. New York: Knopf, 1997.

Wills, Gary. *Inventing America: Jefferson's Declaration of Independence*. Garden City, N.Y.: Doubleday, 1978.

Chapter Fourteen

"War Minus the Shooting"

My daughter Darla was just about to reach the safety of the chorus room when the vice principal of the high school, a squat, dyspeptic woman, busted her for wearing a halter top in violation of the student dress code.

"Come with me," the vice principal said and led the way down the hall. Once inside her closet-like office, she scowled at Darla for what seemed a long time. When she finally spoke, it was to ask in a sharp voice, "Do you play a sport?"

The question secretly struck Darla, who runs as if she were born without full control over her limbs, as hilarious. But when she told me about it after school that day, I wasn't amused. Behind the question lay the widespread belief, more than a century old, that sports build character.

Sports are supposed to teach self-sacrifice, discipline, fair play, and respect for authority. Through sports, kids are supposed to learn to get their kicks on the field or in the gym, and not with drugs and alcohol. If Darla played a sport, the vice principal reasoned, then she was part of the moral elite of the school, someone the rest of the kids can look up to, and wearing the halter top was probably just an innocent mistake. But if she didn't play a sport, who knew what kind of evil freak she was and what other awful deeds she might be contemplating?

There is only one thing wrong with this picture of sports as the salvation of American youth—it isn't true.

Andrew W. Miracle Jr. and C. Roger Rees, who examined forty years of research on tens of thousands of athletes at all levels of competition, found "little empirical evidence that sport builds character or has any positive effects on youth." If anything, most of the research suggested that participation in sports increases "moral callousness." A Canadian study reported, for example, that the longer boys played on youth hockey teams, the more likely they were to accept cheating and violence and to use illegal tactics. Perhaps George Orwell wasn't exaggerating when he said, "Serious sport has nothing to do with fair play. It is bound up with hatred, jealousy, boastfulness, disregard of all rules and sadistic pleasure in witnessing violence. In other words, it is war minus the shooting."

Need more proof that playing a sport might not be the character-building activity many claim it is? Then turn your TV to ESPN or glance through the sports section of a newspaper. What do you find? Colorado Rockies pitcher Denny Neagle, married and with two small children, caught driving around Denver with a prostitute. Swimmer Michael Phelps, six-time gold medal winner at the 2004 Olympics, arrested for drunk driving. Ron Artest, Stephen Jackson, Anthony Johnson, David Harrison, and Jermaine O'Neal, players for the Indiana Pacers, charged with assault and battery after storming into the seats in Detroit and beating up fans.

Moral callousness isn't limited to athletes at the highest levels either. "You think that doesn't trickle down?" Bruce Brown, author of *Teaching Character Through Sport*, asked. He blamed youth league and school coaches who get their concept of what it takes to reach the top from ESPN, then drum it into kids' heads.

A recent survey of 4,200 high school athletes, conducted by the Josephson Institute of Ethics, tends to bear him out. Although 90 percent of the athletes said their coaches set a good example of fair play and sportsmanship, it wasn't clear they knew what a good example was. Large percentages endorsed questionable actions by coaches, from arguing with an official in order to influence future calls to instructing players how to illegally hold and push opponents without getting caught to using a stolen playbook of another team.

Perhaps most troubling, the athletes were inclined to apply "game reasoning"—i.e., if you aren't caught bending the rules, nothing wrong happened—to non-sports situations. Fifty-six percent of males and 45 percent of females agreed with the statement, "In the real world, successful people do what they have to do to win even if others consider it cheating," while 43 percent of males and 27 percent of females agreed with the statement, "A person has to lie or cheat sometimes in order to succeed." The "person" might as well have been the athletes themselves. Sixty-eight percent of both males and females admitted to cheating on a test in school in the past year.

The Duke of Wellington famously declared that the Battle of Waterloo was won on the playing fields of Eton. Commenting on the survey results, Michael Josephson, the institute's president, said, "It appears that today's playing fields are the breeding grounds for the next generation of corporate pirates and political scoundrels." Josephson assumed, just like the Iron Duke, that sports build character, but was far less optimistic about the kind of character under construction. He saw the survey as showing that a malignant, do-whatever-you-gotta-do-to-win coaching philosophy had seeped into high school sports and left the athletes "floating in moral relativism and self-serving rationalizations."

Despite all the evidence to the contrary—doping scandals, research findings, O. J.—most people still believe that sports have a positive effect on character (and, what's more, on their kids' chances for a college scholarship). As Jay Coakley, a sports sociologist at the University of Colorado–Colorado Springs, noted, "There are just so many things vested in those beliefs. People have used them in decisions on how to raise their kids, have spent hours, years watching sports, have funded them through their tax monies. It's really hard to abandon this line of thinking." To criticize high school sports, or to suggest that school taxes might perhaps be better spent on textbooks and teachers, can cause people to look at you with alarm, as if they suddenly suspect you of belonging to an Al Qaeda sleeper cell.

The sacredness of high school sports practically guarantees worship of the "jocks" who play them. Is anyone the least bit surprised that studies have found that male athletes are at the top of the status hierarchy in most high schools? Researchers could have saved themselves work by watching 1980s teen movies, which, no matter how exaggerated they seem in other regards, are remarkably accurate when it comes to portraying the power relations among school cliques. The jocks, effortlessly handsome and surrounded by a gaggle of sexy cheerleader girlfriends, are always shown reigning over the "brains," the "band fags," and the "burnouts" with the casual sadism of medieval lords.

This kind of behavior may be entertaining in movies, but in life, it can be disastrous.

In August 2003, at a football camp in Pennsylvania, three varsity players on Long Island's Mempham High School football team sexually assaulted three junior varsity players at night and in between practices as part of an initiation. (A grand jury later said the five coaches who chaperoned the trip were "more concerned with being coaches of a football team than interested in the well-being of the players.") Often as many as a dozen teammates watched and cheered while the victims were held down and sodomized with pine cones, golf balls, and a broomstick. ("The coaches displayed a lack of common-sense accountability when it came to managing or running the camp," the grand jury reported. "It is unfortunately abundantly clear that the coaches did not know that the crimes committed by their players were being perpetrated.") Duct tape and loud rock music muffled the victims' screams.

After the attacks became public knowledge, some criticized the school for allowing the chief culprit, a junior named Ken Carney, to attend the camp despite a long disciplinary record. Carney once cursed out the umpire at a baseball game, then shouted and swore at his coach. Another time he made a sexual threat in class against a female teacher. It seemed to his teammates that Carney could get away with anything.

"We build athletes up as the symbolic protectors of school and community pride," Miracle and Rees observed, "treat them like demigods, sometimes place them above the laws of the school and community, and then shake our heads in confusion and disbelief when they occasionally call our bluff." The mixed local reaction to the Mempham scandal was a case in point. At school, other students teased the victims, calling them "broomstick boy" and "butt pirate." Three people who spoke out against the coaching staff received death threats in the mail. And though the Bellmore-Merrick Central High School District canceled the Mempham football season and fired the coaches, residents grumbled about it.

Compared to the nightmarish events at the football camp, what happened this fall in my school district may seem almost trivial. Student athletes, who sign a pledge not to use tobacco, alcohol, or drugs, held a party one Saturday night at a motel across the river. Hulking football players drank and mingled with nimble soccer players, preppy tennis players, stoic cross-country runners, and bouncy cheerleaders. When the party started to get out of hand, spilling into the lobby and parking lot, the desk clerk had second thoughts. He picked up the phone and called the police.

By the end of school Monday, news of the party had leaked back to coaches and administrators. The athletic director asked the police across the river for the names of the students who had attended the party, but, like petulant kindergartners, they refused to share. So the district launched its own investigation.

First, every coach met with his or her team and passed around a sheet of paper, ordering anyone who had attended the party to sign it. Those who were honest (or stupid) enough to put their names down were then hauled into the AD's office, where they were pressured to squeal on whoever else was there. The district, in other words, turned as if instinctively to some of the cruelest, most infamous practices of authoritarian regimes—self-denunciation and snitching.

Although the AD ended up with a long list of names, no one was actually kicked off a team, the prescribed punishment for breaking the pledge. To suspend so many players would have meant having to cancel the rest of the fall sports season, a step the district wasn't prepared to take.

Allowing the sports season to go on had the effect of reinforcing the split between the straight, conformist behavior of the athletes in public—for example, wearing a tie to school on game day—and their drunkenness and promiscuity in private. Even worse, it may have given them the feeling that they were somehow bulletproof, immune from the usual penalties and repercussions of rule-breaking. At its extreme, this sense of invulnerability can lead to serious crimes—such as shoving a golf ball dipped in Mineral Ice, an external ointment used for sore muscles, up a fourteen-year-old boy's ass.

You may have concluded from everything I have written so far that I hate sports. I don't. In high school, I ran cross-country and track, and later, as a parent of four growing kids, I coached Little League and youth soccer. Baseball has always been my favorite sport to play or watch, and I especially enjoyed teaching nine- and ten-year-olds who had just gotten their first mitts how to go back on a fly ball and stay down on a grounder.

But sports per se don't build character. As Joel Fish, author of *101 Ways to Be a Terrific Sports Parent*, said, "It's not automatic that if you throw a uniform on a kid, he'll learn life skills." He may learn the exact opposite—cheating, lying, and bad sportsmanship. No one who has studied the issue seems to doubt that sports have the potential to facilitate moral development. For sports to actually do it, though, would require what researchers Sharon K. Stoll and Jennifer M. Beller called "a vastly different coach methodology and participation environment." That is, coaches would have to make character building, rather than winning, their first priority.

The pledge that the student athletes in my district must sign has a preamble full of lofty assurances about the positive nature of high school sports. It claims that the sports program is "an extension and integral part of the total educational curriculum." It urges "all concerned with athletics" to "recognize that the purpose of athletics is to promote the physical, mental, moral, social, and emotional well being of the individual players." It states, "Sportsmanship reveals character and should be emphasized at all times." But saying these things isn't the same as doing them, and saying them without doing them sets the wrong example for kids.

Those athletes who went to the party at the motel let down their coaches and school. They shouldn't have been there, and they sure as hell shouldn't have been drinking. But, by the same token, the adults in charge of the school and its sports program let down the athletes. Whatever lesson the adults intended to teach—and I assume it wasn't something morally toxic—what they did teach was promise-breaking, snitching, and smug indifference to threats of punishment. If the whole episode had been a game, it would have been an oddly joyless one, unfolding on a gray day before a chilled crowd and according to no discernible rules, and the score would have been nothing-nothing when play, already many hours long, was halted on account of darkness.

REFERENCES

Couch, Greg. "Character Study: Money a Bad Influence on Sports." *Chicago Sun-Times*, http://www.suntimes.com/cgi-bin.

Fish, Joel, and Susan McGee. *101 Ways to Be a Terrific Sports Parent: Making Athletics a Positive Experience for Your Child.* New York: Fireside, 2003.

Miracle, Andrew W., Jr., and C. Roger Rees. *Lessons of the Locker Room: The Myth of School Sports.* Amherst, N.Y.: Prometheus Books, 1994.

"New Survey Shows High School Sports Filled with Cheating, Improper Gamesmanship, and Confusion about Sportsmanship." Sportsmanship Survey 2004, http://charactercounts.org/sports/survey2004/.

Schuster, Karla, and Keiko Morris. "Appalled and Sickened." Newsday.com, http:www.newsday.com/sports/highschool/ny-limeph11370324,mar11,0,5936367.

Stoll, Sharon K., and Jennifer M. Beller. "Do Sports Build Character?" in *Sports in School: The Future of an Institution*, ed. John R. Gerdy. New York: Teachers College Press, 2000.

Chapter Fifteen

The Finger

Something made me glance in the rearview mirror while waiting at the stoplight. In the car behind me, I saw a heavy young woman with blonde ringlets, a kind of bloated version of Sarah Jessica Parker, giving me the finger.

I quickly looked back over my shoulder to confirm what I had seen. Sure enough, she had thrust her big, enflamed face close to the windshield and was jabbing her middle finger at me. But why? I hadn't cut her off, and I never ever drive too slowly.

Then I remembered the red, white, and blue bumper sticker my seventeen-year-old daughter, Brittany, had stuck on our minivan. "Be Patriotic," it said. "Vote Bush Out!" The woman apparently didn't appreciate ironic humor. When the light changed, she pulled out around me and screeched away.

The more I thought about the incident over the next few days, the more disturbing it became. I kept seeing in my mind's eye the woman's savage face and her angry middle finger. A story in the news that same week reinforced just how easily and abruptly public discourse can break down. During a concert at the Aladdin hotel-casino in Las Vegas, singer Linda Ronstadt praised *Fahrenheit 9/11*, the documentary by Michael Moore that skewers the Bush administration for invading Iraq. Her remarks caused a near riot. Some of the 4,500 people in the audience only booed, but others stormed out of the theater, tore down concert posters, and tossed drinks in the air. "It was a very ugly scene," Aladdin President Bill Timmins told the Associated Press. He added to the ugliness by kicking Ronstadt off the premises.

Of course, my getting the finger and Ronstadt getting the boot are trivial compared with what happens in many other countries, where rival factions settle their differences with car bombings and assassinations. For me to bemoan the fact that some woman gave me the finger at a stoplight may seem, considering the political, religious, and ethnic violence that torments most of the world, kind of ridiculous.

But perhaps no more ridiculous than ignoring the spread of intolerance and incivility among Americans would be. "Democratic society," educator Deborah Meier pointed out, "depends on our openness to other ideas, our willingness to suspend belief long enough to entertain ideas contrary to our own." Shooting strangers the bird or tearing down posters hardly qualifies as the democratic impulses of an open mind. For democracy to even have a chance of working, we need to first agree to listen civilly to each other, however much we may dislike what we will hear.

The principle is best summed up for me by Tobias in the novel *Tristram Shandy*. Annoyed by a fly buzzing around the room, Tobias finally catches it. He could crush the fly in his fist. Instead, he releases it out the window, saying, "The world is large enough for both of us."

A number of educators, including Meier, Nel Noddings, Susan Ohanian, and Alfie Kohn, have suggested that schools should teach not simply tolerance, which is a passive virtue, but kindness, which is an active one. By kindness these educators mean what is also often meant by "empathy"—"the ability to put yourself in someone else's shoes, the ability to reach out and touch their lives, the ability to care for them."

From what my own kids tell me, just about the last thing you can expect to learn at school is how to be caring. You learn how to cut class without being caught and how to participate in class without being considered a brownnose. You learn how to do homework in the least possible time and how to get good grades with the least possible effort. You learn how to avoid individual responsibility and how to appease adult authority. You learn, in other words, how to navigate the system, which is no small skill. But it has nothing to do with caring.

In fact, we probably couldn't have created a worse system for cultivating the ability to care. Teachers are too busy or burned out to model caring in their relationships with students. Character education is more show than substance. School days are increasingly shaped by the pressures of federally mandated testing. And then we profess concern that today's youth have the moral demeanor of street thugs and blame MTV and violent video games.

Of all the negative factors at work, the most insidious may be overtesting. Not only does it consume huge tracts of time that could be put to better use, it also promotes a certain narrow-mindedness, a kind of mental rigor mortis. To do well on tests requires, obviously, knowing the right answers; you must be able to retrieve on demand specific bits of information stored in your head. But to live civilly with others, you must be able to accept that there can be more than one answer to a question, and that multiplicity and difference represent advantages rather than mistakes.

It isn't that long a step from thinking you have the right answer to thinking you have the right to enforce that answer. In the summer of 2004 the Ten Commandments monument, banned from Alabama's state judicial building as unconstitutional, toured the country on the back of a flatbed truck. First stop was the courthouse in Dayton, Tennessee, where eighty years earlier high school teacher John Scopes was convicted of teaching evolution—the infamous "Scopes Monkey Trial."

About seventy-five people came out to see the monument and pose for photos beside it. Larry Darby, president of the Atheist Law Center, also attended. Some in the crowd shouted, "You're not welcome here," and Darby responded, "That's typical Christianity. These people are the lunatic fringe." A seventy-three-year-old named John Rocco, who claimed to believe in the Ten Commandments, bumped Darby as they passed on the ramp to the monument. "I'm glad I didn't carry my gun," Rocco later said. "I'd probably be in jail right now." In case you forgot, the Second Commandment is Thou Shall Not Kill.

Americans once gathered in coffeehouses, on village greens, and at lyceums to debate the issues of the day. Those places have vanished, but public debate hasn't. Out on the road, I see people expressing their most ardent beliefs and opinions with Jesus fish, Confederate flag decals, "Support Our Troops" magnets. Although what I see sometimes burns my blood, the world is large enough for all of us, hawks and doves, gays and straights, whites and blacks and browns, Christians and Jews and Hindus and Muslims. We just have to remember—and remember to teach our children—to respect, if not each other's opinion, then the right to hold it. Perhaps even when it is held with a middle finger.

REFERENCES

Meier, Deborah. "Supposing That . . ." *Phi Delta Kappan* 78 (December 1996): 271–76.

Ohanian, Susan. *One Size Fits Few: The Folly of Education Standards.* Portsmouth, N.H.: Heinemann, 1999.

Chapter Sixteen

The Way of the Kayak

About five years ago, looking for something that would take my mind off my school board duties, I began kayaking. I've paddled Black Creek, Tivoli Bay, and other estuaries of the Hudson River, coming within arm's reach of wild swans and great blue herons and slipping around beaver dams and down mazes of water lilies. My hours out on the water have suggested to me certain lessons that you might find useful. Here are some:

1. You can paddle against the current and still get where you want to go.
2. Just because you can't see below the surface doesn't mean something down there won't stop you with a jolt.
3. If it doesn't fit on top or inside, you probably don't need it.
4. Everyone could use three things: a whistle to blow in emergencies, a dry bag to protect important stuff, and an anchor to keep from drifting away.
5. You can't ever go anywhere out of the ordinary if you're afraid to get a little wet.
6. The smoother the water, the slower the passage.
7. A person has the right to float once and awhile.
8. Life vests are like most relationships—outfitted with too many straps and buckles.

9. Sometimes you must lean to the right, sometimes to the left in order to keep to the middle.
10. It's good to have a compass, but better to have a sense of direction; it's good to have the wind at your back, but better to have a destination.

Chapter Seventeen

After Story Hour

I sensed the culture might be in trouble when a woman walked into my favorite used bookstore, Tim's Books in Hyannis, and asked Tim, "Is this a library?" Just a few minutes later, the bell over the door jangled again and another woman entered, wearing one of those yellow Gloucester fisherman hats, though it was perfectly dry and sunny out.

"I'm looking for a book," she told Tim.
"What's the title?" he asked.
"I don't know."
"Who's the author?"
"I don't remember."

If I could have avoided witnessing all this, I would have, for it triggered an unfortunate series of questions in my head; namely: Are people really as stupid as they sometimes seem? Is "stupid" even the right word to describe them? Is "bizarre" more accurate? Or am I being overly critical? And what kind of culture produces people who can't remember the title and author of a book, but can recite the name of every runner-up on *American Idol*?

These weren't questions to which I expected any answers. Nonetheless, I may have recently gotten one. It took the form of a study titled "Reading at Risk," released by the National Endowment for the Arts (NEA) and based on a Census Bureau survey.

The study found that less than 47 percent of American adults had read literature (novels, short stories, poetry, or plays) in 2002, down from 54 percent a decade earlier. Reading fell for almost all demographic groups—men and women, young and old, black and white, college graduates and high school dropouts.

But the decline was sharpest among the youngest people surveyed, eighteen- to twenty-four-year-olds. Only 43 percent of them had read any literature in 2002, down from 53 percent in 1992. Apparently, they have never heard Mark Twain's famous line that "the man who does not read good books has no advantage over the man who can't read them." Hell, there is a chance, given the state of our schools, that they have never even heard of Mark Twain.

Why the loss of readers? What happened to the preschoolers who used to happily attend story hour at the local library with their moms? How did so many of them grow up to become such dedicated nonreaders?

The study blames intense competition for readers' time from television, movies, the Internet, and digital devices. When you consider that two-thirds of American children eight and older have a TV in their bedrooms and spend about seven hours a day peering at the screen of some kind of electronic media, the blame seems well-placed.

But there may be more behind the decline in reading than the all-consuming relationship that teenagers and young adults have developed with their cell phones. Ironically, schools may also be responsible for discouraging reading.

I began to suspect this back when I was president of a school board. The No Child Left Behind Act had just gone into effect, and the elementary school principal had come to a meeting to discuss ways of coping with the tough new standards. Under the heavy-lidded gaze of the board, he reviewed, among other things, reading goals for second graders, mentioning mastery in word analysis, vocabulary, and comprehension. But it was what he didn't mention that struck me.

Nowhere in his long, tediously detailed presentation did he say anything about fostering a love of reading. The goals were all technical in nature—"identifying and producing consonant blend and digraph sounds," "expanding sight word vocabulary through appropriate word lists," "increasing the use of multiple meanings." Why shouldn't second graders grow up to hate reading? You would grow up to hate it, too, if you were taught to read not so you can enjoy stories or revel in the play of ideas, but so you can demonstrate on a state test your skill in "identifying grade-level appropriate word families."

Schools tend to operate on the elitist assumption that not everyone is a reader—that, in fact, many students have an innate dislike for reading and must be driven, sometimes with bribes (grades, certificates, etc.), sometimes with threats, to read at all.

Aristotle, although he lived in a slave society, had a more generous view of people's potential. "Learning something is the greatest of pleasures not only to the philosopher," he said, "but also to the rest of mankind, however small their capacity for it." It is the delicious and inimitable pleasures of reading that should be emphasized at school. Instead, teachers assign extra reading as punishment.

Being both a professor of writing and a professional writer, naturally I'm worried about the disappearance of readers. Writing has always been an insecure profession; just think of Herman Melville, after the commercial flop of *Moby Dick*, lamenting, "Though I wrote the Gospels in this century, I would die in the gutter." But now I wonder whether it will become a vestigial one as well. Will writers someday be as curious figures as blacksmiths and coopers are, dressed up in antique clothes and exhibiting their quaint art to sightseers at a living museum?

Perhaps writers aren't the only ones who should be worried. The NEA study noted that a decline in reading foreshadows declines in other activities. Nonreaders are less likely than readers to do volunteer and charity work, participate in sports, and attend cultural events. When people stop reading, or never truly start, a few more strands in the community fabric unravel.

There may even be an increased danger to our basic freedoms. At the height of the Cold War, Robert M. Hutchins, then president of the University of Chicago, saw lack of reading as a threat to democracy at least on par with Soviet communism. "To lose the tradition of independent thought," he warned, "it is not necessary to burn books. All we have to do is leave them unread for a couple of generations."

Television, movies, and the Internet may have many pluses, but one of them isn't the encouragement of more thoughtful modes of being. Reading helps us develop intellectual resources that the electronic media, for all their wonderful convenience, can't. As Dana Gioia, chairman of the NEA, put it, "Print culture affords irreplaceable forms of focused attention and contemplation that make complex communications and insights possible." A culture in which people stop reading runs the risk of reverting to a kind of wilderness, a chaos of brutal gestures, simplistic slogans, and rampant, disconnected images.

I suppose I should thank you for reading all the way to the end of this when you could be watching TV or talking on your cell phone. But before you go, I need something explained to me. Why is it that, with millions fewer readers around than ten years ago, I still can't ever seem to find a close-in parking space at Barnes & Noble?

REFERENCES

Hutchins, Robert M. *The Conflict in Education in a Democratic Society.* New York: Harper & Brothers, 1953.

"Literary Reading in Dramatic Decline, According to National Endowment for the Arts Survey," NEA News Room, http://www.nea.gov/news/news04/ReadingAtRisk.html.

Chapter Eighteen

Write and Wrong

What should I say to college students who can barely write an intelligible sentence? How does "Get the hell away from me" sound?

It probably sounds a little harsh to you. But, to my ears, it sounds like a solution. That's because two decades of reading student writing may have finally caught up with me, like a state trooper with a hard face and an unfilled ticket quota.

Back when they were in grade school, my students learned to read and write phonetically. It's a teaching method that doesn't even look good on paper. There they mistake "feudal" for "futile," "ladder" for "latter," "which craft" for "witchcraft." There they write, "The room smelled like incest," when they mean to write—at least I hope they mean to write—"incense."

As someone once observed, it's a good thing children learn to speak before they start school. Otherwise they would all grow up to be either mutes or stutterers.

My students' writing stutters like the failing engine of a doomed plane. I can quote whole paragraphs from their papers that don't make sense, that fill the passenger cabin with smoke and toxic fumes.

But why subject you to all the terrifying things I must endure, the aborted takeoffs and crash landings? I'll just quote a typical sentence: "Some moral principles that need to be followed are philosopher Immanuel Kant's idea about the maxim of protecting someone who cannot protect them is a maxim that could be universalized." I warned you there might be turbulence and to keep your airsick bag handy.

It has occurred to me that students might learn to write better if they wrote more often—you know, practiced. But this apparently hasn't occurred to anyone else.

Statistics released in 2003 by the National Commission on Writing in America's Schools and Colleges show that two-thirds of high school seniors write English papers less than once a month and that three-quarters have never received a writing assignment in history or social studies. The commission also reported that fourth graders spend about 85 percent more time each week watching television than they do writing.

In the past, I would have found these numbers alarming. Not anymore. Now I consider it almost fortunate that kids watch so much TV. It means they aren't off in a corner committing unnatural acts with the mother tongue.

You may be wondering by this point what someone with my attitude is doing in a classroom. I'm doing what I've always done. When I'm not searching for a piece of chalk, I'm preaching the rules of good writing.

Literary authorities from A (well, O, George Orwell) to Z (William Zinsser) generally agree that the rules are as follows: keep it simple; be specific; pick a suitable design and hold to it; don't use a long word when a short word will do; don't use images you're accustomed to seeing in print; have the guts to cut; swear by the little verbs that bounce and run and swim; sound like yourself; revise, revise, and then revise some more.

I preach these rules as earnestly as ever, just not as hopefully. If hope is, as the poet said, "a thing with feathers," I'm feeling pretty well plucked.

I wish I felt differently. I wish I felt that all the recent commotion about improving public education and leaving no child behind was having a positive effect. I wish I felt that the students coming out of high school could write a sentence without impaling themselves.

But I don't. I'm overwhelmed by the feeling that writing is a lost art and that rediscovering it isn't exactly a cultural priority.

It shouldn't be a surprise, then, that when students approach my desk with their papers, I want to scream, "Get the hell away from me!" Somehow I restrain myself. I smile and nod and even murmur, "Thank you . . . thank you . . . thank you," while I collect their papers and stuff them in my briefcase.

Later at home, I attack each paper with a kind of controlled fury, my pen slashing through the clotted prose like a jungle machete. I simplify sentences, reword awkward or murky phrases, fix grammar and usage, circle clichés, cut redundancies, until the page is crowded with my corrections and revisions, and it isn't just their work anymore, but, I suddenly realize, ours.

Chapter Nineteen

Sing!

I hear my daughter singing. The door to her room is closed, but I can hear Darla behind it trying out a Gershwin classic, "Someone to Watch Over Me." She has a lovely voice, full of vibrato, as if she were pulsing with adult emotions.

This is all a bit surprising. Darla had belonged to chorus since fourth grade, but almost indifferently, the way most people belong to a book club. Then the high school hired a new chorus teacher, a young woman recently out of college, who noticed Darla hidden among the altos and praised her voice and encouraged her to refine it.

Now Darla hangs out in the chorus room during lunch period and after school, and when she comes home, she practices her songs without having to be reminded. At dinner she doesn't ever talk about Earth Science or English, unless it's to complain that there's a test or a lot of homework, but she's always chattering about the song selections for the next concert and who's up for a solo and what Ms. Ruiz, the chorus teacher, said.

It's nice that Darla has found at least one thing at school to get excited about. It must be nice for the chorus teacher, too. Without Darla and some other kids like her, school would probably be unbearable for Ms. Ruiz, a tedious hell of discipline problems and cafeteria duty and paperwork.

Bel Kaufman perfectly captured in her 1963 novel, *Up the Down Staircase*, the small victories on which a teacher's sanity can depend. The narrator, first-year teacher Sylvia Barrett, confesses, "Whenever I feel too frustrated to go on, I find an unexpected compensation: a girl whose face lights up when she enters the room; a boy who begins making sense out of words on a printed page; or a class that groans in dismay when the end-of-period bell rings."

These are what are sometimes called "the intrinsic rewards of teaching." Intrinsic rewards are necessary because teaching has so few extrinsic ones—you know, like money or status.

The lack of extrinsic rewards has caused the kind of people who used to go into teaching—"high-aptitude women," in the phrase of educational researchers—to generally not go into it anymore. They can now go into better-paying, more prestigious professions, such as medicine, engineering, finance, and law. Teacher and author Ted Sizer was only half-joking when he recently said, "We could solve the teacher quality problem overnight. All we have to do is take away all opportunities for women to have other jobs."

Or prevent new teachers from leaving the jobs they already have. About 30 percent of new teachers quit teaching after three years, and more than 45 percent after five.

Researchers have compiled a long list of reasons why teachers say they quit. Many cite low salaries, but even more complain about poor working conditions.

Vivian Troen and Katherine C. Boles contend in their book, *Who's Teaching Your Children?*, that teachers endure "the worst working conditions of any so-called professional." Most, they point out, "have no telephones, no fax machines, no personal computers, and only limited access to copiers."

The very buildings in which teachers work can be an obstacle to job satisfaction. Bel Kaufman's description of a fictional but typical urban high school, Calvin Coolidge, is as depressingly accurate today as it was when she wrote it more than forty years ago: "cracked plaster, broken windows, splintered doors and carved up desks, gloomy corridors, metal stairways, dingy cafeteria." The National Education Association estimates that 60 percent of all schools in America need major repairs.

Another reason teachers give for leaving is little to no administrative support. Almost two-thirds of former teachers in North Carolina indicated in a survey that a lack of administrative support was a factor in their departure.

Still other teachers quit out of fear for their safety. Esmé Raji Codell, who eventually left classroom teaching to become a school librarian, taught in a neighborhood plagued by gangs and drug-related violence. As she recounts in *Educating Esmé*, her diary of her first year of teaching, she used to wonder, "Will I be shot by a student? So many of them have guns at home. Why will I be shot? For suspending, scolding, letting someone cut in line, for giving too much homework?"

Teachers also say they leave because they feel inadequately prepared for the pressures of teaching, because they're inundated with extracurricular duties, because they're assigned to the most-difficult-to-teach students or to courses outside their areas of expertise, because they have few opportunities for advancement, and because they suffer from loneliness and isolation.

Given all this, perhaps the question to ask isn't why do so many teachers leave, but why do any of us stay. And yet we do.

Last spring a graduating senior gave me a chunk of crystal with a quote from Henry Adams etched on it: "A Teacher Affects Eternity. He Can Never Tell Where His Influence Stops." She gave it to me mostly as a thank-you, but also, she said, to remind me not to lose hope when my classes seemed hopeless.

Good teaching is hard work. It may look easy, like anyone can do it, but not just anyone can. You've got to concentrate, you've got to practice, and perhaps you need an inborn talent, the soul of an artist.

As a young man, I had no intention of making a career out of teaching. I wanted to be a writer, and teaching just seemed more sensible than stealing car stereos to support my twice-a-day writing habit. But a teacher is what I've primarily become, at least according to my income tax returns. On the line that asks my occupation, my accountant doesn't put Writer–Teacher. He puts Teacher–Writer. Most days I can live with that.

Other people sell kids stuff that's ugly or unnecessary or that may hurt them, either now or twenty years from now. Other people exploit them, scare them, pack them off to war. I don't. I teach them.

Of course, I can't always find the right key to unlock their curiosity about a subject. I search my key ring, my painfully acquired set of classroom skills, but the key may not be there or, if it is, I may not recognize it. When that happens, I brood and fret and feel like the world's worst failure.

But when the key fits, oh, wow.

It doesn't matter then that the classroom clock is broken or that there aren't enough books to go around. It doesn't matter that the state keeps changing the curriculum or that the department chair has the ethics of a cannibal. It doesn't even matter that the pay is bad. All that matters is that a teacher is asking questions, and the students are asking questions back, and they're learning to think for themselves and finding out that it's not only important, but also—just look at the sparkle in their eyes!—a joy.

REFERENCES

Codell, Esmé Raji. *Educating Esmé: Diary of a Teacher's First Year.* Chapel Hill, N.C.: Algonquin Books of Chapel Hill, 1999.

Curran, Bridget, and Liam Goldrick. "Issue Brief: Mentoring and Supporting New Teachers." Education Policy Studies Division, National Governors Association for Best Practices, January 9, 2002.

Kaufman, Bel. *Up the Down Staircase.* Englewood Cliffs, N.J.: Prentice-Hall, 1963.

Troen, Vivian, and Katherine C. Boles. *Who's Teaching Your Children?* New Haven, Conn.: Yale University Press, 2003.

Chapter Twenty

Board-dom

It's two years since I last served on the school board, and I don't want to go back to it, ever.

I'm not the only one to feel this way. Gary Lister, a school board member from Georgia, has compiled an e-book, *99 Reasons to Never, Ever Again Run for School Board*, with contributions from current and former board members from around the country.

So what if there are actually only fifty-four reasons given? (No. 4: "Education gobbledygook intrudes into your conversations.") The overall point is still valid—school board service can be traumatizing.

In fact, I seem to exhibit some of the classic symptoms of post-traumatic stress disorder, including nightmares, flashbacks, and extreme distress from personal "triggers."

I can't sleep after I attend one of my daughter's school events. I become agitated whenever I read an article in the paper about the district. Even worse, if I happen to bump into a current board member, or an antagonist from my former days as board president, I feel an unhealthy impulse to gouge out their eyes.

You wouldn't know it from my bitter state of mind, but the only thing I ever wanted to do during my six years on the school board—six years of arguing, compromising, begging, dreaming, and, most of all, meeting—was help kids.

Of course, that's not what current board members say.

"You'll never guess what they say about you!" my last remaining friend on the board exclaims.

That I fornicated with the goats at Wilklow's (a farm next to the high school)?

Pretty much.

I once believed that, as Anne Bryant, executive director of the National School Boards Association, put it, "In a democracy, school boards are the closest thing to the ground." Now I believe that school boards spend most of their time dealing with minutiae—hiring (or firing) the football coach, screening textbooks, listening to complaints about school bus stops.

Am I being too harsh? There may be only one way for me to find out—attend some school board meetings.

I cringe at the prospect. And can you blame me? If you'd narrowly escaped death in a cave-in, you wouldn't hurry to return underground either.

But, with a long, sad sigh, I shoulder a pick and shovel, switch on my headlamp, and descend once again into the cold darkness.

* * *

Actually, it's the high school library. The school board meets there the second and third Tuesday nights of every month.

Many of the items on the agenda are familiar from my own days on the board—resignations, child-rearing leaves, teaching appointments, director reports. It's not exactly the stuff dreams, or blue-ribbon schools, are made of.

I suppose it doesn't help either that school business is often conducted in a kind of secret code. At one point during the meeting, the director of pupil personnel services, a woman of quite normal appearance, tells the board, "We'll be able to run off our PD-fives, -sevens, and -eights in the next week," and then mentions the "CSPE" and the "citation in the four-o-five."

Board-dom

Whatever language she's speaking, it isn't English. I'm not sure it's even human.

Things eventually liven up when the board turns to item 7b, "Final Discussion and Approval of the Athletic Code of Conduct." Several months ago, word circulated through the district that varsity athletes from the fall sports teams had held a drinking party at a local motel. If true, this violated their signed pledge not to use alcohol, tobacco, or drugs.

But the athletic director, despite a strenuous investigation, couldn't get the athletes to incriminate themselves or snitch on each other. Board members were outraged that the party animals had eluded capture. They ordered the AD to form a committee to revise the athletic code. It's that revision they'll approve tonight.

Only they don't.

"This just doesn't do it for me," the board president says with a frown. "I'd have to up the ante for the first offense."

You mean like sticking the heads of student athletes who violate the code on poles outside the high school?

As if reading my mind, the superintendent says, "I think the school should be about teaching kids. We shouldn't throw kids away."

The president's frown deepens. "I don't think in this area we should give second chances."

A board member who's known for his mild manner says, "We asked them to form a committee to make a new policy. I don't think we should send them a mixed message and go back to the old policy." But he says this so mildly that he doesn't sound entirely convinced of it himself.

"How come there weren't people on the committee?" the vice president of the board asks. The other board members ignore her, probably because the question makes no more sense to them than it does to me.

Instead, the only other woman on the board says, "I was never really in favor of adopting a new policy. I think the old policy was strict, and I'm perfectly comfortable with that. Athletes need to be held to a higher standard."

The superintendent tries again to break the board's fixation with punishment. "Sometimes kids make mistakes," he says. "When they do, it's an opportunity to teach them."

"Why don't we give 'em polygraph tests?" the vice president suggests. "Ask 'em, 'Did you smoke a cigarette this week?'"

"It's the athletic department's failure to enforce the existing rules that's been the issue," the other woman board member says, "not the policy."

The last board member now speaks up. "I'm against the old policy and the new policy," he announces.

I glance at the superintendent. His face is a blank. He knows from past experience that the board will go round and round for the next half hour and then decide not to decide anything yet.

Although I don't particularly trust him—like most superintendents, he's as much a politician as an educator—I almost feel sorry for him.

* * *

A week after attending my first school board meeting in two years, I have a strange dream.

In the dream, I arrive at the high school at about 7 p.m., just as the light is filtering from the sky. I get out of my car and walk to the main doors, but though a board meeting is scheduled for that night, the doors are locked. I bang on the glass with my fist, no one comes. I then look around more closely and discover that my car is the only car in the parking lot.

Suddenly, I'm sitting in a red vinyl booth in the diner with the longest-serving board member, a building contractor who, in the dream, resembles pro wrestler-cum-Minnesota governor Jesse "The Body" Ventura. "Uh, yeah," he says in a slow, dunce-like voice, "you missed the meeting." The board apparently did meet at the high school at 7—7 in the morning! I realize without Jesse Ventura saying it that the meeting time was moved to avoid having me there.

Dawn is still a couple hours away when I struggle awake, astonished at how extensive my paranoia has become. Then again, raging paranoia may be the only appropriate response to the fact that the local public schools have been entrusted to the cast of the World Wrestling Federation.

REFERENCE

Elizabeth, Jane. "School Board's Worth in Doubt." *Pittsburg Post-Gazette* (November 30, 2003), http://www.post-gazette.com.

About the Author

Howard Good (B.A., Bard College; M.A., University of Iowa; Ph.D., University of Michigan) is a professor of journalism at SUNY New Paltz and a former president of the Highland (N.Y.) school board. A frequent contributor to *American School Board Journal*, *Education Week*, and *Teacher Magazine*, he has written ten previous books, including *The Theory of Oz: Rediscovering the Aims of Education* and *Educated Guess: A School Board Member Reflects*. He has also edited a volume of essays, *Desperately Seeking Ethics: A Guide to Media Conduct*, and written a chapbook of poetry, *Death of the Frog Prince*. His book-in-progress, *Gathering Fuel in Vacant Lots: Stories of Miseducation*, will be published by Rowman & Littlefield Education.

www.ingramcontent.com/pod-product-compliance
Lightning Source LLC
Chambersburg PA
CBHW031714230426
43668CB00006B/204